HEART OF JOY

Heart of Joy

Mother Teresa

Edited by José Luis González-Balado

SERVANT BOOKS
Ann Arbor, Michigan

Cover photograph by de Wildenberg/Sygma
Cover design by Michael Andaloro

Words taken from Scripture, when identifiable, have
been taken from the New American Bible.

Published by Servant Books
P.O. Box 8617,
Ann Arbor, Michigan 48107

Printed in the United States of America
ISBN 0-89283-304-1

92 93 94 95   10 9 8

Contents

Introduction

SOME WHO READ these pages may find them somewhat disordered and repetitious. Some repetitions might have been avoided; the order might have been different; the tone might have been more consistent. But we ask our readers: Would you prefer a very ordered book or an authentic book? For the truth is that something more polished would have been, in this case, less authentic.

It is only fair to confess that not everything that appears in these pages has been written by Mother Teresa for a book. We should actually say that she has not written anything for a book. All these things have been written, explained, and said by her, but she has done so for her sisters, for the co-workers of her mission, in private conversations, in more or less formal lectures, in interviews, and in press conferences.

Mother Teresa is not an author. Rather, she is a person who lives and works intensely. She is a person who lives—and who gives up her life!—on behalf of others. Those others are the poorest of the poor.

It is others of us who, driven by the power of Mother Teresa's witness, are trying to make sure that the echo of her words is stronger, that the sweeping force of her example is manifest. That is why we have gathered these more or less casual yet intimately sincere words of Mother Teresa and have given them the shape of a book. Our desire is that her words may be an encouragement for many—and for ourselves!—to benefit Christ's poorest poor.

Mother Teresa is already one of the best-known persons of our day. Prestigious television programs and newspapers have featured her. Best-selling magazines have dedicated lively cover stories to her life and work. Various biographies have helped make her better known—biographies in English, French, Spanish, Italian, German, Portuguese, Swedish, Hungarian, and so on. She has been awarded some of the most famous international prizes, among them the Nobel Prize for Peace.

This book, born of the desire to make known the words that have been lived by Mother Teresa before they were ever uttered or written, is indebted to many collaborators. The two names heading the list are Mrs. Ann Blaikie, director of the international Co-workers of Mother Teresa, and Georges Gornée, who was director of the French *Amis de Mère Teresa* until his death.*

I am also especially grateful to Jesús Prada and Janet Playfoot de González. The first of them took care of final drafts for many of the texts that make up the book. Mrs. Playfoot de González was very patient in transcribing from the original English cassettes.

My most sincere gratitude goes to all of these people, as well as to all those who read these pages and promote them.

---

*Abbe Georges Gornée, tireless promoter of Mother Teresa's work, with whom many of us had a deep friendship and to whom we were indebted, died of a heart attack on January 15, 1977. God has surely rewarded this man's commitment to works of charity.

ONE

The Generosity
of the Poor

*The following text is adapted from the address of Mother
Teresa in Philadelphia on August 6, 1976, on the occasion of
the International Eucharistic Congress. This talk was
included in the symposium "Freedom and Justice," in which the
Brazilian Bishop Dom Helder Camara and Fathers Arrupe
and Haring also intervened.*

It is now seven hundred and fifty years since St. Francis of
Assisi composed the following prayer for himself and for
those whom he taught to love God:

> Lord, make me an instrument of your peace.
> Where there is hatred, let me sow love.
> Where there is injury, let me sow pardon.
> Where there is friction, let me sow union.
> Where there is error, let me sow truth.
> Where there is doubt, let me sow faith.
> Where there is despair, let me sow hope.
> Where there is darkness, let me sow light.
> Where there is sadness, let me sow joy.

O Divine Master, grant that I may not so much seek
to be consoled as to console,
to be understood as to understand,
to be loved as to love,
For it is in giving that we receive.
It is in pardoning that we are pardoned.
It is in dying that we are born to eternal life.

God loved the world so much that he gave to it his Son
Jesus as the beginning of Christianity. Jesus became like
us in everything except sin. And this was his recom-
mendation to us: "Love one another as I have loved you."

How did Jesus love us? He became living bread that
you and I might eat, that we might live. He became so
small and so weak in order to meet our hunger for God.
Bread, just bread, the simplest of all food to the point that
even a child can eat it and understand it. He changed it
into his own body and said, "If you do not eat the flesh of
the Son of Man and drink his blood, you have no life in
you."

Jesus needed the body of Christ in order to love his
Father, in order for the two of them to love each other.
The kindness of Christ's love was hungry for your love
and mine. He wanted to meet his hunger for our love, and
so he became hungry, naked, dispossessed, so that you
and I could see him, touch him, serve him.

That is why I say that my sisters and brothers, the
Missionaries of Charity, are not social workers: they are
contemplatives in the midst of the world. Their lives are
consecrated to the Eucharist through contact with Christ
under the appearance of bread and under the sorrowful
countenance of the poor.

In order to help us deserve heaven, Christ set a
condition: that at the moment of our death you and I
whoever we might have been and wherever we have lived,
Christians and non-Christians alike, every human being

who has been created by the loving hand of God in his own image shall stand in his presence and be judged according to what we have been for the poor, what we have done for them.

Christ said, "I was hungry and you gave me food." He was hungry not only for bread but for the understanding love of being loved, of being known, of being someone to someone. He was naked not only of clothing but of human dignity and of respect, through the injustice that is done to the poor, who are looked down upon simply because they are poor. He was dispossessed not only of a house made of bricks but because of the dispossession of those who are locked up, of those who are unwanted and unloved, of those who walk through the world with no one to care for them.

Do we go out to meet those? Do we know them? Do we try to find them?

The Generosity of the Poor

The poor do not need our compassion or our pity; they need our help. What they give to us is more than what we give to them.

I have a memory of the terrible days we underwent when millions of refugees were fleeing to India; I asked the Indian government to allow some religious sisters from abroad to come and help us serve the refugees. Many came, about sixteen or seventeen, from various religious orders. They spent six months with us, offering love, service, tenderness, and care to those who needed it. When they left, all of them said that what they had received was much more than what they had been able to give.

Several months ago—as you know, we work also by night—we went through the streets of Calcutta and picked up four or five persons. Given their conditions, we took them to the House of the Dying. Among them was an old woman who was very seriously ill. I said to the sisters, "I will take care of her."

When I laid her on the bed, she took my hand, and a wonderful smile appeared on her face. She uttered one single word, "Thanks," and she died.

This woman gave me much more than I gave her. She offered me her grateful love.

Just for a second I stared at her and wondered, "What would I have done in her place?" I answered to myself, "I would have done all I could to attract attention to myself. I would have cried, 'I'm hungry,' 'I'm cold,' or, 'I'm dying.'" She instead was so great, so splendid in her generosity.

The poor—I'll never get tired of saying this—are wonderful.

Do We Know the Poor?

A few weeks before my trip to the United States, someone came to our house by night and said, "There is a Hindu family with eight children, and they have gone several days without eating."

I took a bit of rice and went immediately to their assistance. The mother took the rice from my hands, distributed it into two equal servings, and went out immediately.

When she came back I asked, "Where have you been? What have you been doing?"

"They are hungry too," she answered.

Right next to them lived a Muslim family with the same number of children. The Hindu mother knew they had been out of food for several days. She did what Jesus does: she broke the bread. She broke her love and shared it with her neighbors.

I cannot describe to you the faces of those youngsters.

When I went in, I knew they were suffering. I could see their little faces. I could see their eyes shining because of hunger. When I left, their eyes were shining with joy because both the mother and the children were able to share their love with others.

What impressed me most in that instance was that the woman *knew*. Do we know our poor people? Do we know the poor in our house, in our family? Perhaps they are not hungry for a piece of bread. Perhaps our children, husband, wife, are not hungry, or naked, or dispossessed, but are you sure there is no one there who feels unwanted, deprived of affection? Where is your elderly father or mother?

One day I visited a house where our sisters shelter the aged. This is one of the nicest houses in England, filled with beautiful and precious things, yet there was not one smile on the faces of those people. All of them were looking toward the door.

I asked the sister in charge, "Why are they like that? Why can you not see a smile on their faces?" (I am accustomed to seeing smiles on people's faces. I think a smile generates a smile, just as love generates love.)

The sister answered, "The same thing happens every day. They are always waiting for someone to come and visit them. Loneliness eats them up, and day after day they do not stop looking. Nobody comes."

Abandonment is an awful poverty.

On one of our nightly walks through London, I discovered a teenage boy, with long, well-groomed hair. He was sitting, thinking.

I said to him, "You shouldn't be here at this time. You should be with your parents. This is not a proper place for you to be at this time and on such a cold night."

He stared at me and said, "My mother doesn't want me because I have long hair."

There was no other reason. A young man, a mere

teenager, rejected by his own people, by his own mother! I reflected for an instant: "Maybe his mother is concerned about the hungry people in India, in Africa, or in the third world. Maybe she desires to meet the needs of all except her son. She doesn't know that poverty, hunger, exists in her own house. It is she who provokes such hunger."

That's why I ask: "Do we know our poor people? Do we know how poor we ourselves are?"

A nation that destroys the life of an unborn child, who has been created for living and loving, who has been created in the image of God, is in a tremendous poverty. For a child to be destroyed because of the selfishness of those who fear they may not be able to feed one more child, fear they may not be able to educate one more child and so decide that the child has to die—that's poverty.

"I Was Ill . . ."

I like to repeat: "The poor are very kind people. The poor are great. They have great value. They give to us much more than we give to them."

In many places we have houses for the dying. I remember the day I picked up a woman in the street, thinking that she was starving to death. I offered her a dish of rice. She kept looking at it for a long while. I tried to persuade her to eat.

Then she said, with utter simplicity, "I can't believe it's rice. I have been a long time without eating."

She condemned no one. She did not complain against the rich. She did not utter any bitter words. She simply couldn't believe it was rice.

Yes, the poor are great. We have to love them, but not with pity love. We have to love them because it is Jesus who hides under the likeness of the poor. They are our brothers and sisters. They belong to us. The lepers, the dying, the starving, the naked—all of them are Jesus.

That is what one of our sisters experienced. She had just entered our group, right after finishing her college studies. One morning she had to go with another sister to the House of the Dying.

Before they went I told them, "You know that you have to go there. During the mass (we have mass before going to work every morning) think with what tenderness, with how much love, the Father treated the body of Christ. Be persuaded that it is the same body that you will touch in the poor. Give them the same love, the same tenderness."

The sisters went. Three hours later they were back. The new sister came up to my room to tell me, "Mother, I have been touching the body of Christ for three hours." Her face was shining with joy.

I asked her, "Sister, what is it that you have done?"

She explained, "As soon as we arrived they brought a man full of worms. They had picked him up in a sewer. For three hours I have been touching the body of Christ. I know it was he."

That sister understood that Jesus cannot mislead us. He has said, "I was ill and you comforted me."

The Freedom of Poverty

Our sisters and brothers, in order to be able to do what they do, commit themselves to love Christ with undivided heart in chastity, through the freedom of poverty, in obedience, and in total service to the poorest poor. In order to be able to lead this life, we have to love the Eucharist very much.

With Jesus we start our walk every day. As we come back at sunset, we have an hour of adoration in the presence of Jesus exposed in the Eucharist. The ten or twelve hours of service to the poor that we carry out every day suffer no interruption because of this.

The hour of adoration is the greatest gift God could

offer to a community. It draws us close to one another; we love each other more because of it. Above all, I think it enables us to love the poor with a deeper faith and a greater love.

Pray for us sisters, that we may never frustrate the work of God.

As I read the gospel, I cannot but smile at those who tell us that we are spoiling the poor in offering them our free service. I think no one has given us more than God has, who has given us everything freely. And it is not so bad to have at least one congregation that spoils the poor, when everybody else spoils the rich.

I am deeply impressed by the fact that before explaining the word of God, before presenting to the crowds the eight beatitudes, Jesus had compassion on them and gave them food. Only then did he begin to teach them.

What Our Lady does is similar: at the moment Jesus entered her life, at the very moment when—so to speak— she made her first communion, Mary hurried to go and serve Elizabeth. And what did she do? She became the handmaiden of the Lord.

We too—you and I—have to begin by giving Jesus to others. People nowadays suffer much, but above all they are hungry for God.

Our novitiate is full to overflowing. You should see the letters I receive from young people, even from your own children here in the United States! In the last two months alone we have received more than fifteen young people.

They are determined to give up everything. One of them, a girl from a well-to-do family, wrote to me: "I desire it. Jesus is calling me. Jesus has chosen me. I desire to commit myself fully to God. Wherever I look I see that what I have they also have. If I join them, there's nothing for me to lose."

Young people love renunciation. They desire to experience the freedom of poverty, freely chosen.

In our community we choose poverty: we want to know the poor, to understand them. To that end we have to know what poverty is all about.

Our poverty is the result of a choice. That is why I speak of the freedom of poverty. We have the freedom to love God, to love Jesus, and to love the poor, all with an undivided heart.

St. John says, "If anyone says 'My love is fixed on God,' yet hates his brother, he is a liar" (1 Jn 4:20). Therefore, both you and I, let us turn our eyes to our own families, since charity begins at home. Do we really understand the poverty of Christ, the poverty of our poor, of our home, of our communities?

Sometimes it is hard for me to smile at my sisters. It is easier to smile at those outside than to smile at our own.

With Deep Gratitude

I am here in the name of the poor, of our poor. I want to thank you, people of the United States, for the love and generosity you have shown toward them. From the very beginnings of our congregation—we are still a young congregation—Catholic Relief Services has channeled your love, your help, your sacrifices, on behalf of our poor.

With deep gratefulness, in their name, in the name of the invalid and the unwanted, in the name of the dying and the hungry, of the lepers and of alcoholics, in the name of all of them and in my own name, in the name of my sisters and brothers, I thank you for the love and generosity that you have shown throughout these years.

One thing I ask of you: never be afraid of giving, but do not give your surplus. Give to a point that is difficult for you. Jesus felt wounded as he loved you and as he loved me. There is a deep joy in giving, since what we receive is much more than what we give.

The same happens with the Eucharist. We receive Jesus himself in the bread, which is the bread of life. And he offers us the beautiful opportunity to give him back what he gives us.

Never turn your back on the poor, for if you do so you are turning your back on Christ Jesus. Every day, after holy communion, we sisters recite the following prayer, which was composed by Cardinal Newman:

Dear Jesus,
Help me to spread your fragrance wherever I go.
Flood my soul with your Spirit and life.
Penetrate and possess my whole being so utterly
that my life may only be a radiance of yours.
Shine through me and be so in me that every soul I
   come in contact with
may feel your presence in my soul.

Let them look up,
and see no longer me,
but only Jesus!
Stay with me and then I will begin to shine as you shine,
so to shine as to be a light to others.

The light, O Jesus,
will be all from you; none of it will be mine.
It will be you, shining on others through me.
Let me thus praise you in the way which you love best,
by shining on those around me.
Let me preach you without preaching, not by words
   but by example,
by the catching force, the sympathetic influence of
   what I do,
the evident fullness of the love
my heart bears for you. Amen.

In remembrance of the Eucharistic Congress, and as a gift to the people of the United States, on June 25, the feast of the Sacred Heart, the contemplative branch of the Missionaries of Charity was offered to the Sacred Heart by Cardinal Cooke, Archbishop of New York. We trust that these sisters, the Sisters of the Word, will be able to live the word of God in adoration and contemplation and to proclaim it to the poorest poor.

Pray for us.

For our part, I deeply thank you for the love, kindness, and generosity that you have shown toward us, toward each one of us, toward all the poor of the world. We will pray for you.

May you make of your homes another Nazareth. May Jesus be able to come and rest, to bring peace, love, and joy to your hearts and to your homes.

God bless you all.

TWO

Jesus, Mary, and Us

Following is Mother Teresa's address on the topic "Women and the Eucharist," given at the Forty-first International Eucharistic Congress in Philadelphia, August 7, 1976.

Dear co-workers of Christ:

I believe that our mother the church has elevated women to a great honor in the presence of God by proclaiming Mary the Mother of the Church. God so loved the world that he gave his Son. This was the first Eucharist: the gift of his Son, when he gave him to Our Lady, establishing in her the first altar.

Mary was, from that instant on, the only one who was able to affirm with complete sincerity, *This is my body.* She offered her body, her strength, her whole being, to form the body of Christ.

It was on her that the power of the Holy Spirit rested, and in her that the Word became flesh. Mary gave herself to him completely because she had previously consecrated herself to him—in order to preserve her virginity virgin, her purity pure, and her chastity chaste, and in order to offer them to the only living God.

When the angel announced to Mary the coming of Christ, she only posed a question: she could not understand how she could take back the gift of herself that she had made to God. The angel explained it, and she understood immediately. Her lips uttered a beautiful response that asserted all that she was as a woman: "I am the servant of the Lord. Let it be done to me as you say."

"They Have No More Wine. . ."

Our Lady—the most beautiful among all women, the greatest, the most humble, the purest, the holiest—in the moment when she felt flooded by grace, full of Jesus, ran in haste.

I think this is why God chose a woman to show his love and compassion toward the world. It was she, the woman, who gave evidence of her kindness by immediately sharing what she had just received. To say it in another way, she hastened to share the Eucharist.

We know well what happened to John the Baptist in the womb. In the presence of Christ he leaped for joy.

This is our gift as women. We have been created to be the center and the heart of the family.

As St. Therese of the Child Jesus once said, "I want to place myself in the heart of the church in order to offer love." You and I have been created for that same end: for loving and for that love, as Mary did everywhere and at all times.

We too have to go look for our children, just as Mary did when Jesus was lost. We must live through the worry of not knowing where our children are. The home is not a home without the child. We also discover the genuine Mary, full of tenderness, in the wedding feast at Cana. She was moved by seeing the newlyweds exposed to the humiliation of not having wine. That is why she said to Jesus, "They have no more wine."

I think this is the wonderful tenderness of a woman's heart: to be aware of the suffering of others and to try to spare them that suffering, as Mary did. Do you and I have that same tenderness in our hearts? Do we have Mary's eyes for discovering the needs of others?

Perhaps in our own homes: Are we able to perceive the needs of our parents, of our husband, of our children? Do our children come home with us, as Jesus went home with Mary his mother? Do we offer our children a home?

We know what happened to Mary, the mother full of tenderness and love who was never ashamed of proclaiming Jesus her son. Eventually everyone abandoned him. Mary stayed beside him.

Mary was not ashamed by the fact that Jesus was scourged, that his face was spit upon, that he was treated as a leper, as one unwanted, despised, hated by all. Because he was Jesus, her son. And there surfaced the deep tenderness of her heart as a mother.

Do we know how to stay beside our own in their suffering, in their humiliation? When our husband loses his job, what do we represent to him? Do we feel tenderness toward him? Do we understand his anguish?

When our children are pulled away from us and receive bad advice, do we feel that deep tenderness that makes us go after them in order to draw them toward us, to welcome them kindly in our home, and to love them with all our heart?

Am I like Mary for my sisters in the community? Do I realize their suffering, their sorrows?

If I am a priest, do I have a heart like Mary's? Do I experience the tenderness of forgiveness? Can I offer God's forgiveness to the humbled sinner who stands before me?

"The Greatest Gift of God to Us"

Mary did not feel ashamed. She proclaimed Jesus her son. At Calvary we see her standing upright—the mother of God, standing next to the cross.

What a deep faith she must have had because of her love for her son! To see him dishonored, unloved, an object of hatred. Yet, she stayed upright.

As the mother possesses her son, she possessed him, knowing that he who belonged to her was at the same time her absolute master. She was not afraid to accept him as her belonging.

Do we know how to consider our own as our belonging when they suffer, when they are discarded? Do we acknowledge our own as our family when they suffer? Do we realize the hunger they have for Jesus in the hunger they feel for a love that understands them?

This is the source of Mary's greatness: her understanding love. You and I who are women—do we possess that great and magnificent thing, that love full of understanding?

This is the love I observe with amazement in our people, in the poor women who day after day discover suffering and accept it because of their love for their children. I have seen many fathers and mothers deprive themselves of many things—very many!—and even beg, in order for their children to have what is needed. I have seen fathers affectionately carry their abnormal children in their arms because those children are their own. I have seen mothers full of a very tender love toward their children.

I remember a mother of twelve children, the last of them terribly mutilated. It is impossible for me to describe that creature. I volunteered to welcome the child into our house, where there are many others in similar conditions.

The woman began to cry. "For God's sake, Mother," she said, "don't tell me that. This creature is the greatest gift of God to me and my family. All our love is focused on her. Our lives would be empty if you took her from us."

Hers really was a love full of understanding and tenderness. Do we have a love like that today? Do we realize that our child, our husband, our wife, our father, our mother, our sister or brother, has a need for that understanding, for the warmth of our hand?

The Love of Small Things

My sisters also work in Australia. On the reservation, among the Aborigines, there was an elderly man. I can assure you that you have never seen a situation as difficult as that poor old man's. He was completely ignored by everyone. His home was disordered and dirty.

I told him, "Please, let me clean your house, wash your clothes, and make your bed."

He answered, "I'm okay like this. Let it be."

I said again, "You will be still better if you allow me to do it."

He finally agreed. So I was able to clean his house and wash his clothes. I discovered a beautiful lamp, covered with dust. Only God knows how many years had passed since he last lit it.

I said to him, "Don't you light that lamp? Don't you ever use it?"

He answered, "No. No one comes to see me. I have no need to light it. Who would I do it for?"

I asked, "Would you light it every night if the sisters came?"

He replied, "Of course."

From that day on the sisters committed themselves to visiting him every evening. We cleaned the lamp, and the sisters would light it every evening.

Two years passed. I had completely forgotten that man. He sent this message: "Tell my friend that the light she lit in my life continues to shine still."

I thought it was a very small thing. We often neglect small things.

Hungry for God

Some time ago our sisters in Rome came across someone in very sorrowful circumstances. He was one of those persons who are locked up in themselves, with no contact with the surrounding society.

I think the sisters had never seen anything like that. They washed his clothes, cleaned his room, prepared some hot water for him. They left everything ordered and clean. They even prepared some food for him. He was still mute; he was not able to utter a single word.

The sisters decided to go to his house twice a day. A few days later he broke his silence to say, "Sisters, you have brought God to my life. Bring me also a priest."

That man made his confession, after sixty years. The next day he died. This is beautiful. The tenderness of those young sisters carried God to that man, who for many years had forgotten what God's love is, what loving each other means, what it means to feel loved. He had forgotten it because his heart had closed itself to everything.

The humble, simple, tender work of the young sisters was the tool God used to enter the life of that poor man. But what impressed me most was the greatness of the priestly vocation; that poor man needed a priest in order to come into contact with God.

I believe that what we can learn from Our Lady is her tenderness. All of us, you and I, have to use what God has given us, that for which he has created us.

God has created us for great things: to love and offer love, to experience tenderness toward others, as he did, and to know how to offer Jesus to others. People are not hungry for us; they are hungry for God. They are hungry for Jesus, for the Eucharist.

In 1976, at the invitation of the President of Mexico, we opened a house in that nation. Our sisters, as is the custom in our congregation, were full of activity—seeing everyone, walking tirelessly until their legs could endure no more, trying to discover where the greatest need was in order to begin there.

They found deep poverty everywhere in Mexico. All the zones they visited appeared immensely poor. But no one asked them for clothing or medicine or food—nothing. Only, "Teach us the word of God."

I was very surprised. Those people are hungry for God: "Teach us the word of God."

They didn't know the sisters; they had never seen them. But they saw that the sisters carried rosaries in their hands, and they thought about that.

When we walk the streets, in whatever part of the world, the sisters carry in their hands the crown of the rosary. The Virgin is our strength and our protection. I can assure you that throughout all these years the younger sisters have been penetrating the most difficult places without being touched by anyone.

Even in New York, although it is said that we have been in the most difficult district of the city these past five years, I can assure you with complete honesty that the sisters have never had to hear a discourteous word. As they pass, there are no sarcastic comments. No one has ever put their hands on them or caused them the least harm. The greatest respect and dignity have always accompanied them, even though they enter ruined houses, inadequate for habitation. They enter places where others cannot easily enter.

The Virgin always protects us. She is the cause of our joy, and we try to be a cause for her joy. Thus gathered, following her example, invoking her protection, staying united with her, we can move through the most difficult places with no fear at all because Jesus is with us and he will never abandon us: Jesus is our love, our strength, our source of kindness.

God has created women for this. Perhaps he didn't create them to do great things, but certainly at least to do small things with a great love. And I believe that this love is to begin in the home, coming from our hearts; in our families with our neighbors, next door, with our neighbors on the next street. And then it must be extended to all.

Only thus will we be able to extend the meaning of the Eucharist. The meaning of the Eucharist is love that understands. Christ understood. He understood that we are terribly hungry for God. He understood that we have been created for loving.

That is why he became the bread of life. And he said, "If you do not eat my flesh and drink my blood, you will not be able to live. You will not be able to love. You will not be able to serve" (see Jn 6:53).

We have to eat him. The kindness of Christ's love is his love that understands.

Christ wants to offer us the means of putting our love for him into action. He becomes hungry, not only for bread but for love. He becomes naked, not only for a piece of clothing but for love that understands, for human dignity. He becomes dispossessed, not only for a place of shelter but for the sincere and deep love for one another.

This is what the Eucharist is all about. This is Jesus, the living bread that has come to be broken with you and with me.

I think that the greatest love and honor we can demonstrate to Our Lady may be to stand up and recite the Angelus:

MOTHER TERESA: The angel of the Lord declared unto Mary.

RESPONSE: And she conceived of the Holy Spirit.

MOTHER TERESA: Hail, Mary, full of grace, the Lord is with you. Blessed are you among women, and blessed is the fruit of your womb, Jesus.

RESPONSE: Holy Mary, Mother of God, pray for us sinners, now and at the hour of our death. Amen.

MOTHER TERESA: Behold the handmaid of the Lord.

RESPONSE: Be it done unto me according to your word.

MOTHER TERESA: Hail, Mary . . .

RESPONSE: Holy Mary . . .

MOTHER TERESA: And the Word was made flesh.

RESPONSE: And dwelt among us.

MOTHER TERESA: Hail, Mary . . .

RESPONSE: Holy Mary . . .

MOTHER TERESA: Pray for us, O holy Mother of God,

RESPONSE: That we may be made worthy of the promises of Christ.

MOTHER TERESA: Let us pray. Pour forth, we beg you, O Lord, your grace into our hearts; that we to whom the incarnation of Christ your Son was made known by the message of an angel, may by his passion and cross be brought to the glory of his resurrection. Through the same Christ our Lord. Amen.

THREE

The Cross
of the Poor

*This is Mother Teresa's meditation for youth at the Stations of
the Cross, on the occasion of the International Eucharistic
Congress in Philadelphia, August 5, 1976.*

> *Lord, make us worthy to serve men, our brothers, who are
> dispersed all over the world, who live and die in poverty and
> hunger. Give to all of them, through our hands, their daily
> bread, and through our understanding love give them peace
> and joy.*

Jesus said to the youth of his day, "If you want to be my
disciples, take up your cross and follow me" (see Mt
16:24).

Jesus knew that we needed him, that we would not be
able to follow him, to carry our crosses on our own. He
became the bread of life. He told us that unless we ate his
flesh and drank his blood, we would not have life, we
would not be able to follow him. We would not be able to
be his disciples.

Even though he no longer needs to take up his cross
and walk toward Calvary, today—in you, in me, in the
youth of our world—Jesus continues to endure his

passion. The small child, the child full of hunger who eats his bread crumb by crumb because he is afraid of running out of bread before running out of hunger—that is the first station of the cross.

Am I able to see the poor and suffering? We often look without seeing. All of us have to carry our own cross, all of us have to accompany Jesus in his ascent to Calvary if we want to reach the summit with him.

Jesus, before his death, gave us his body and blood so that we could live, so that we could have strength, so that we would have life and would be able to drag our cross and follow him step by step.

In our way of the cross we see Jesus, poor and hungry, enduring his own falls. Are we there to offer him our help? Are we there with our sacrifices, with our piece of bread, of real bread?

There are thousands of people dying for a piece of bread. There are thousands upon thousands who die for a little bit of love, for a little bit of acknowledgment. This is one station of the cross: Jesus present in those who are hungry and falling under the weight of the cross.

In the fourth station of the cross Jesus meets his mother. Are we mothers for those who suffer—mothers full of love, of understanding? Are we there with our ability to offer understanding to young people when they are burdened, when they are alone, when they feel rejected? Are we there?

Simon of Cyrene began following Jesus when he helped him bear his cross. That is what you young people have done throughout this year as a symbol of your love: thousands and thousands of things you have offered Jesus in the poor. You have been genuine Cyrenians each time you have carried out one such action or gesture.

Are we like Veronica to the poor, toward those who lie prostrate in their loneliness, toward those who feel rejected?

Are we there to wipe away their sorrow? Are we there to share their suffering? Are we there, or are we rather like the proud man who passes by, glances at the one in need, and continues on his way?

Jesus falls again. How many times we have picked up in the streets human beings who had been living like animals and were longing to die like angels!

Are we there to help the needy get up? Are you able to see the people sunning in the parks, who feel alone, undesired, unattended, immersed in sadness? They are Jesus, and he needs your hand to wipe his face. Are you there to do that, or do you walk away?

Jesus fell again, once more, for you and for me. He was stripped of his clothes.

Today small beings are deprived of love even before birth. They have to die because we do not want one more child. That child has to be left naked because we do not want him.

Jesus bore that unspeakable suffering. This unborn child bears it because no other possibility is offered him. But I can want him, love him, care for him. This child is my brother, my sister.

Jesus is crucified. How many human beings who are handicapped or mentally retarded, even in their young age, are filling the hospitals! How many of them there are, even in our own homes!

Do we ever visit them? Do we ever go to share with them the hour of their crucifixion? Do we even know them?

Jesus told us, "If you want to be my disciples, take up my cross and follow me." He meant that we should carry the cross and feed him in those who are hungry; that we should clothe him in those who are naked; that we should host him in our home, treating him as a brother.

Let us begin our way of the cross with cheer and joy because through Holy Communion we have Jesus with us. We have Jesus, the bread of life, who gives us life and strength. His joy is our strength, and his passion is also our vigor. Without him we can do nothing.

You young people, full of love and strength, do not waste your energy on useless things. Look and see your brother and your sister, not only here in the United States, not only in your city or your area. Everywhere there are human beings who are hungry and who look to you. There are naked human beings who look hopefully to you. There are dispossessed people who look to you. Do not turn your back on the poor because the poor are Christ.

FOUR

What It Means to Be a Co-worker

This is an excerpt from the Co-worker Newsletter, published in Minneapolis, spring 1977.

I hope we can all grow in love for one another just as Christ loves us. What I desire in a special way is for us to deepen our mission, our life, and our prayer. Ours is a mission of love and kindness, especially today, when men are so hungry for God.

I have but one concern: that all of us may be co-workers of Jesus. You know it well: a Missionary of Charity is a messenger of God's love. I trust that in time each co-worker will also become a messenger of God's love. But in order to achieve that, we ought to deepen our life of love, prayer, and sacrifice. It is very difficult, if not impossible, to give Jesus to others if we don't first have him in our hearts.

If we really want to be co-workers of Christ, we have to accept Jesus. We have to accept his love and his compassion. We have to be willing, as Mary was, to give Jesus to others.

We ought to be bearers of peace, love, and compassion for today's world. In order to do that, we need neither cannons nor bombs. We only need a deep love, a deep union with Christ, in order to be able to give him to others. Compassion and love have to grow inside us out of our union with Christ.

The co-worker is the life of Christ shining in today's world. Before we can live that life outside, we have to live it in our own homes.

In today's world there are many sorrows, and I feel that most of those sorrows come from the family. There is ever less unity in the family, less prayer, and less fellowship. And there is less time together.

As co-workers, you are offered a wonderful opportunity and a great mission to live that life of peace and unity, and through that to proclaim to the world that Christ is alive.

Co-workers are spread all over the world. Some of them are well-known, others aren't. I do not want co-workers to become one more organization, a welfare group busy with fund-raising. The co-worker is a person with a mission—a mission of love that comes only from union with God. And out of that union flows, as a natural fruit, love for the family, love for one's neighbor, and love for the poor.

Our eucharistic union with Christ has to bear that fruit because Jesus said, "I am the vine, you are the branches" (Jn 15:5). The fruit is borne by the branch, not by the vine. Hence the great responsibility you and I have since the fruit depends on the union of the branch and the vine. I would like the fifteenth chapter of John's Gospel to become our life.

The congregation of the Missionaries of Charity is the branch, and all the co-workers are small branches united to Jesus, who is the vine. I think this is the most expressive image of what each one of us should be in the world.

In order to be able to take this love and compassion to those who need us, we need prayer and sacrifice. In order or your service to the poor to continue being really a service to the poor, it must be maintained on a basis of sacrifice.

There are so many sorrows in today's world! These sorrows are due to hunger, to dislodging, to all kinds of illnesses. I am convinced that the greatest of all sorrows is to feel alone, to feel unwanted, deprived of all affection. It consists in not having anyone, in having gotten to the point of forgetting what human contact is, what human love is, what it means to be wanted, to be loved, to have a family.

Therefore, let us deepen our love of Jesus. Let us deepen our knowledge of God. This knowledge will lead us to love him, and love will lead us to serve him.

Let us offer all this work for the glory of God. May we all be instruments of peace, of love, and of compassion.

FIVE

Christianity Is Giving

Following is Mother Teresa's address at the university parish of Cambridge, England, June 10, 1977, when she was awarded the honoris causa *doctorate by the Duke of Edinburgh, Chancellor of that university.*

To the question, What is Christianity? a Hindu gentleman answered, Christianity is giving.

God so loved the world that he gave his Son. He gave him to Mary, that she would be his mother. Jesus became a person, just as you and I, except without sin. And he showed his love to us by giving us his life, his whole being.

He made himself poor though he was rich—for you and for me. He gave himself up completely. He died on the cross. But before dying he became the bread of life—in order to meet our hunger for love.

He said, "If you do not eat the flesh of the Son of Man and drink his blood, you have no life in you" (Jn 6:53). The greatness of his love made him feel hunger. And he said, "I was hungry and you gave me food. If you do not give me food, you cannot enter eternal life" (see Mt 25:31-46).

Such is Christ's gift. God continues to love the world in

our day. He sends you and me to show that he still loves the world and that he has not stopped having mercy on it. It is we who today have to be his love and mercy to the world.

But in order for us to be able to love we need to have faith because faith is love in action, and love in action is service. This is why Jesus became the bread of life: so that we may be able to eat and live and to see him in the faces of the poor. In order for us to be able to love we have to see and touch. And so Jesus made the poor the hope of salvation for you and for me. In fact, Jesus said, "As often as you did it for one of my least brothers, you did it for me" (Mt 25:40).

The Missionaries of Charity are not social activists but contemplatives in the very heart of today's world. We take literally the words of Jesus: "I was hungry, I was naked, without a home, and you gave me food, you clothed me, you gave me shelter" (see Mt 25:35-36). In this way we are in contact with him twenty-four hours a day. This contemplation, this touching of Christ in the poor, is beautiful, very real, and full of love.

Our poor do not need compassion or condescendence: what they need is love and aid. But we have to be aware that the poor are worthy of love, that they are great. This will lead us to love them and serve them.

Love Begins at Home

Do we know our poor here and now? There may be poor within our own family: let us not forget that love begins at home. Do we know them? Do we know those who live alone? The unwanted? The forgotten?

One day I found among the debris a woman who was burning with fever. About to die, she kept repeating, "It is my son who has done it!"

I took her in my arms and carried her home to the convent. On the way I urged her to forgive her son. It took a good while before I could hear her say, "Yes, I forgive him." She said it with a feeling of genuine forgiveness, just as she was about to pass away.

The woman was not aware that she was dying, that she was burning with fever, that she was suffering. What was breaking her heart was her own son's lack of love.

St. John says, "How can you say that you love God, whom you do not see, if you do not love your neighbor, whom you see?" He uses a strong expression for such an attitude: "You are a liar if you say that you love God but do not love your neighbor" (see 1 Jn 4:20).

I think this is something we all have to understand: that love begins at home. In our day we see with growing clarity that the sorrows of the world have their origin in the family. We do not have time to look at each other, to exchange a greeting, to share a moment of joy. We take still less time to be what our children expect of us, what our spouse expects of us. And thus, each day we belong less and less to our own homes, and our contacts are less.

Where are our elderly people today? Usually in institutions. Where is the unborn child? Dead! Why? Because we do not want him.

I see a great poverty in the fact that in the West a child may have to die because we fear to feed one more mouth, we fear to educate one more child. The fear of having to feed an elderly person in the family means that this person is sent away.

One day, however, we will have to meet the Lord of the universe. What will we tell him about that child, about that old father or mother? They are his creatures, children of God. What will be our answer?

God has invested all his love in creating that human life. That is why we are not entitled to destroy it, especially we who know that Christ has died for the salvation of that life. Christ has died and has given everything for that child.

If we are really Christian, then for us too, as for that

Hindu gentleman, "Christianity is giving." We have to give until it hurts. Love, in order to be genuine, has to have a cost. For Jesus the cost was loving us. Even God had a cost in loving: he gave us his Son.

There's nothing I can give you today because I have nothing. But what I desire from you is that when we look together and discover the poor in our families, we may begin to give love in our homes until it hurts. May we have a prompt smile. May we have time to devote to our people.

A few days ago, a man came toward me on the street and asked, "Are you Mother Teresa?"

"Yes," I answered.

He asked, "Send one of your sisters to our home. I am half blind, and my wife is on the fringe of insanity. We long to hear the echo of a human voice. This is the only thing we miss."

When I sent the sisters, they realized it was true. The couple lacked nothing materially. But they were being suffocated by the anguish of not having any relatives nearby. They felt unwanted, useless, unprofitable— doomed to die in utter loneliness.

This wounds Christ's heart. He loved to the point of suffering. But how will we be able to love the poor if we do not begin by loving the members of our own family?

Love—I will never get tired of saying it—*begins at home*.

God Provides

My sisters are very busy with the poorest poor, with the handicapped, the blind, the abnormal. We have homes for the seriously ill and for the dying.

We are about to celebrate the twenty-fifth anniversary of our House of the Dying in Calcutta. Throughout these twenty-five years we have picked up more than thirty-six thousand seriously ill people in the streets, of whom about sixteen thousand have died among us.

I feel that the most adequate way of commemorating this anniversary is by celebrating it on November 1, the feast of All Saints. I am more than sure that all these people who have died with us are in heaven. They are genuine saints. They are already in the presence of God. Perhaps they were not loved on earth, but they are favorite children of God.

Therefore I want to pray and to thank God for all the beautiful things that my sisters have done in the House of the Dying. Even though that house is a part of the temple of Kali, the goddess of terror, what reigns there above all is the joy of helping the ill to die in peace with God.

You would be amazed to see the calmness with which these people die. One day the sisters picked up a man who was already half eaten by worms. He said, "I have lived in the streets like an animal, but I am going to die like an angel, surrounded by love and care." He really died like an angel, with a very serene death.

Some time ago, we in Calcutta underwent a period when sugar was very scarce. Somehow the story spread that Mother Teresa had no sugar for her orphans.

A child said to his parents, "For three days I won't eat sugar: what I save I want to give to Mother Teresa."

So his parents, who had never been to our house, brought the child with a can of sugar. He was four years old and could barely speak, but that small child had a great love: he loved with sacrifice.

We who know Jesus, who love Jesus, who are even consecrated to Jesus, have to love as Jesus has loved. He has given us the bread of life so that we may love as he has loved us. He continues to say, "As the Father has loved me, I have loved you" (Jn 15:9).

How has Jesus loved us? By giving himself to us. This is how we are to love each other: by giving ourselves to each other, giving ourselves to the point of feeling pain. I don't want you to give me your surplus. I want you to give with personal deprivation.

I and my sisters have deliberately chosen to be poor, depending exclusively on divine providence. It would take me a whole day and night to tell you the thousands of proofs of the loving providence and fatherhood of God toward us. We deal with thousands of people, and we have never had to tell anyone, "We are sorry, but we have run out of everything."

In Calcutta we care for some seven thousand people every day. If one day we don't cook, they will not eat. A sister came to me one day and said, "Mother, there is no rice for Friday and Saturday. We should let the people know." I was surprised because throughout twenty-five years I had never had to hear anything like that.

Friday morning, about nine o'clock, there came a truck full of thousands of small loaves of bread. No one in Calcutta knew why the government had closed the schools that day, but it had happened, and all the bread was brought to us. For two days the people we cared for were able to get enough bread.

I guessed why God had closed the schools: he wanted the people we care for to know that they were more important than grass, than birds, and than the lilies of the field—that they were his favorites. Those thousands of people needed proof that he loved them, that he cared for them. That was a clear proof of God's tenderness toward his children.

Prayer and Sacrifice

In order to be able to carry out her task, every sister consecrates her life to the Eucharist and to prayer. You might be surprised to hear that we have hundreds of young and generous vocations. Young women write to us wonderful things: "I want a life of poverty, of prayer and sacrifice, to go along with my service to the poor."

That's what our young women are like: full of love and
generosity. In a moment they can be sent anywhere, to
carry out the most humble task. We also have brothers—
the Missionary Brothers of Charity—who carry out a task
similar to ours in complete submission to God's will. It is
exciting to see our young people so fully committed,
overflowing in love toward Christ's poor.

Our congregation is fully devoted to feeding Christ
who is hungry, clothing Christ who is naked, aiding
Christ who is ill, offering shelter to Christ who is ousted.
We profess the three vows of loving Christ with undivided love in chastity, through the freedom of poverty,
in total commitment through obedience. We assume a
fourth vow whereby we commit ourselves to offer from
our hearts voluntary service to the poorest among the
poor, that is to say, to Christ under the humble
appearance of the poor.

We need prayers in order to better carry out the work of
God. Pray for us, so that the work we do may be God's
work and so that in every moment we may know how to be
completely available to him.

The ideal of our congregation consists of quenching
the thirst of Christ on the cross for the sake of souls. The
spirit of the congregation is total commitment to God, a
loving confidence in the superiors, and loving care. For
without joy there is no possibility of love, and love
without joy is not sincere and genuine love.

We have to take that love and that joy to today's world.
We have no need of cannons or bombs to bring peace: we
only need love and kindness. And we also need a deep
union with God and prayer—prayer accompanied by
sacrifice, and sacrifice accompanied by adoration.

A family that prays together stays together. As we are
united at this moment, let us join also the prayer of all and
everyone. What you can do I cannot do. And what I can do

you cannot do. But all of us together are doing something beautiful for God.

Let us now pray thus:
Lord, make us worthy to serve our brothers,
men of all the world,
who live and die in poverty and hunger.
Give them this day, through our hands, their daily
    bread.
And through our love and understanding, give them
    peace and joy. Amen.

SIX

God's Call

I was only twelve years old, living with my parents in Skopje, Yugoslavia, when I first sensed the desire to become a nun. At that time there were some very good priests who helped boys and girls follow their vocation, according to God's call. It was then that I realized that my call was to the poor.

Between twelve and eighteen years of age I lost the desire to become a nun. But at eighteen years of age I decided to leave my home and enter the Sisters of Loreto. Since then I have never had the least doubt that I was right. It was God's will: he made the choice.

The Poorest Poor

At Loreto I was the happiest nun in the world. Leaving the work I did there was a great sacrifice. What I did not have to leave was being a religious sister.

The Sisters of Loreto were devoted to teaching, which is a genuine apostolate for Christ. But my specific vocation, within the religious vocation, was for the poorest poor. It was a call from inside my vocation—like a second vocation. It was a command to resign Loreto, where I was happy, in order to serve the poor in the streets.

In 1946, when I was going by train to Darjeeling for

some spiritual exercises, I sensed a call to renounce everything in order to follow Christ in the poor suburbs, to serve among the poorest poor. I knew that God wanted something from me.

The Temptation of Comfort

A shelter was needed to care for those who were abandoned. So I started searching. I walked and walked, until I could not walk any more. Then I understood to what point of exhaustion the real poor have to arrive, always in search of some food, of medicine, of everything. The memory of the material comfort that I enjoyed at the Loreto convent appeared then to me as a temptation.

I prayed:
O, my God,
By free choice and for your sake
I desire to stay here and do what your will requires of me.
No, I will not turn back.
My community is the poor.
Their safety is mine.
Their health is my health.
My house is that of the poor—of the poorest among the poor;
of those one tries to avoid for fear of contagion and dirtiness, because they are covered with microbes and worms;
of those who do not go to pray, because one cannot go out of one's house naked;
of those who do not eat anymore, because they have no strength for eating;
of those who fall down on the streets, knowing that they are going to die, and at whose side pedestrians pass and don't look back;

of those who do not weep anymore, because they have
 run out of tears;
of the untouchable.

The Lord has willed me here where I am. He will offer a
solution.

The Revolution of Love

One by one, from 1949 on, my former students began
to arrive. They wanted to give everything to God, right
away. With what joy they put away their colorful *saris* in
order to put on our poor cotton one. They came because
they knew that it would be hard.

When a young woman of high caste comes and puts
herself at the service of the poor, she is the protagonist of
a revolution. It is the greatest, the most difficult revolution—the revolution of love.

God's Love

The aim of our congregation is to take God, to take his
love, to the homes of the poorest poor and to lead them to
him. It is of little importance who they are, what their
ethnic background is, or what their place in society is. We
want to show them the love and compassion God has for
them. We want to show them that God loves the world
and loves them.

The Temple of the Goddess Kali

The press told the drama of people dying in the streets
without receiving any care whatsoever. I took advantage
of that to convince the municipal government: "Give me a
facility; I will take care of the rest."

They allotted me two halls of the temple of the goddess

Kali, two large rooms which up to that point had been designated as sleeping places for pilgrims. I gladly accepted the facility, as it was a center of Hindu devotion and worship. We immediately moved the ill people there.

The priests of the goddess Kali didn't think favorably of our meddling. But one of them came down with a contagious illness. We took such good care of him that from that time on the priests stopped spying on us and even became our collaborators and friends.

God Loves Silence

The first work we have to do with those who are seriously ill, whom we have often picked up from the streets, is to wash their faces and their bodies. Most of them do not even know what soap is, and they are afraid of a sponge. If the sisters did not see in these miserable people the face of Christ, this work would be impossible for them to do.

We want these poor to realize that there are people who really love them. Here they find again their human dignity, and they die in an impressive silence.

God loves silence.

Serving the Poor

Not even in the early times did I ever ask for money. I wanted to serve the poor exclusively out of love for God. I wanted the poor to receive freely what the rich get with money.

Overflowing Work

All of my time belongs to others. The same happens with the sisters. They work without resting for the sick and for the children. They have no time left, not even for writing a letter.

Tell those who write us not to feel sad if they receive no answer. The work is really overflowing.

A Rare Medicine

Providence always comes to our help. When the need is immediate, the intervention of providence is also immediate. It is not always a matter of huge amounts, but of what is needed at a given moment.

One time we had picked up a man for whom a rare medicine was needed. While we were wondering how we could get it, a man knocked at our door with an abundant sampler of medicines. Among them was the one we urgently needed.

Something That Is Much

I know it well and my sisters know it too: what we do is less than a drop in the ocean. But if that drop were missing, the ocean would lack something.

If we did not have small schools in the poor neighborhoods—and some of those schools are very small— thousands of children would be abandoned in the streets. Our solution can only be to do all we can for them.

The same is true of the people sheltered in our houses for the dying. Most of them die just the same, but it is worthwhile offering them a place where they can find God and die in peace.

Adoptions

There are so many children today who are categorized as undesired, as unwanted. The problem that worries so many people is that the world is beginning to look too populated. What concerns my sisters and me is that people do not think that divine providence can provide for the new ones, for the unborn.

In my opinion, if abortion is allowed in the rich countries, who possess all that money can provide, then those are the poorest among the poor. I would like to open in such countries many houses for children, in order to welcome them and provide what they need. We have many such houses in all of India, and up to now we have never seen the need to reject any child.

The most wonderful thing is that each child who has escaped death by the hands of his parents has later found a home with new parents. For some years now in Calcutta we have been trying to prevent abortions by means of adoptions. Thanks to God, we have been able to offer many who otherwise would have died a father and a mother to love them and to offer them affection and care.

For us in India this is something so wonderful because by law these children are untouchable. One of the most admirable traits of our people is their willingness to offer a home and tenderness to these undesired children, and thus to Christ.

As He Loved Us

We have houses for the abandoned, as in Melbourne, Australia. There we welcome people who have no one, who are wandering through the streets, who only have the street and the tomb.

One man who came to us had been seriously offended by a friend of his. Thinking that the matter was serious, someone asked, "Who was it?" The man resorted to all sorts of lies. It was clear that he would never say the name of the guilty one.

When the other person left I asked, "Why didn't you want to tell the name of the one who hurt you?"

The man looked at me and said, "His suffering wouldn't have diminished mine."

This is what it means, in my opinion, to love each other as he loved us.

Jesus and the Poor

Only by getting closer and closer to Jesus will we be able to get closer to each other and to the poor.

Being Filled with God

The more we become empty of ourselves, the more we will be able to be filled with God.

"You Did It to Me"

May we never forget that in the service to the poor we are offered a magnificent opportunity to do something beautiful for God. In fact, when we give ourselves with all our hearts to the poor, it is Christ whom we are serving in their disfigured faces. For he himself said, "You did it to me."

"Say It Again"

In Calcutta alone we have picked up more than twenty-seven thousand (as of 1973) abandoned people in the streets. They meet us, we welcome them, and we take them to our House of the Dying.

They die serenely, with God. Neither I nor any of the sisters have ever found a single man or woman who has refrained from saying to God, "I repent," or who has not wanted to say, "My God, I love you."

We have thousands of lepers. They are wonderful, they are admirable, even though their flesh is disfigured.

Every year we offer the lepers a Christmas party. Last Christmas I told them that they have a gift from God, that God has a special love for them, that they are very acceptable to God, that what they have is not a sin.

An old man, who was completely disfigured, tried to get close to me. He said, "Say it again. That has been good for me. I have always heard that no one loves us. It is wonderful to know that God does love us. Say it again."

Serenity

What is required of a Missionary of Charity is this: health of mind and body; ability to learn; a good dose of good sense; joyous character.

If one of my sisters is not in at least a serene mood, I do not allow her to go visit the poor. The poor already have so many reasons to feel sad; how could we take them the affliction of our own personal bad moods?

The Light of Christ

We do not intend to impose our faith on others. We only expect Christ to reach out with his light and his life in and through us, to the world of misery. We expect the poor, no matter what their beliefs are, to feel drawn toward Christ as they see us and to invite us to get closer to them, to enter their lives.

Total Self-Giving

The most important thing in my life has been my encounter with Christ: He is my support.

Christ is the love that must be loved, the way that must be trodden, the truth that must be spoken, the life that must be lived, the love that must be loved. That is why we, the Missionaries of Charity, love Christ with undivided love, in total self-giving in chastity, in absolute freedom in poverty, and in full self-surrender in obedience, with exclusive commitment and dedication to the service of the poorest poor.

Faith in God

A Hindu cabinet minister declared at a public meeting that when he saw the Missionaries of Charity working among the lepers, it seemed to him that he was seeing Christ anew on the earth, putting himself at the service of the poor.

An Indian physician, as he saw the care a sister devoted to a sick man who had been declared hopeless by his colleagues, said, "I came here without God. I'm now going back with God."

A Need

Holiness is not a privilege of a few but a need for all.

The Generosity of Young People

I am convinced that today's youth are more generous than those of times past. Our youth are better prepared and more willing to sacrifice for the service of man. For that reason, it is no surprise that young people have a preference for our congregation.

To a large extent these are young people from the middle class. They have everything: wealth, comfort, high status. However, they ask to enter a congregation that is at the service of the poor, in order to lead a life of real poverty and contemplation.

Serving God

If someone feels that God wants from him a transformation of social structures, that's an issue between him and his God. We all have the duty to serve God where we feel called. I feel called to help individuals, to love each human being. It is not my task to judge institutions—I am not competent to judge anybody.

I never think in terms of crowds in general but in terms of persons. Were I to think about crowds, I would never begin anything. It is the person that matters. I believe in person-to-person encounters.

The Heroism of Saints

How pure our hands ought to be if we are to touch the body of Christ, just as the priest touches it under the likeness of bread. With what veneration and love does he lift up the consecrated host! The same should our feeling be every time we touch the body of a sick person.

It was this insight that transformed Father Damien into an apostle to the lepers, that made St. Vincent de Paul the father of the poor. St. Peter Claver used to lick the wounds of the black slaves. St. Francis of Assisi too, when he met a completely disfigured leper, at first wanted to run away but then embraced that horrible face. And this action filled him with unspeakable joy, to the point that the leper went away thanking God for his healing.

Why all this? Because all of these saints wanted to get as close as possible to God's own heart.

Relieving Pain

At the House of the Dying we understand the value of each soul. The very fact that God has placed a soul on our way is a sign that he wants us to do something for it.

As we visit families, we encounter many miseries. Sometimes, we see a small child tenderly caressing the head of his dead mother. Once the sisters came across two children beside the body of their father, who had died two days before. At such times we need all of our energy in order to relieve the immense pain of these poor creatures.

Awards and the Poor

I am but an instrument.

The first time I received an award, I was very surprised. I did not know whether to accept it or not. But I came to the conclusion that I should accept awards in the name of the poorest poor, as a form of homage to them.

I think that basically, when awards are given to me, the existence of the poor in the world is being recognized.

SEVEN

Serving the Poor

These are the words of Mother Teresa to the national delegates of the associations of Co-workers of Mother Teresa in Lippstadt, West Germany, August 15, 1976.

Co-workers of Christ

I want to express to you affection and gratitude, not only mine and my sisters' but also on behalf of the poor to whom both you and we devote our care.

An encounter such as this one should be an occasion for us to grow to love each other as Jesus loves you and loves me. I want each one of you to grow in the sense of our spiritual mission of love and of a life of prayer.

Our mission is a mission of love. It is a mission of kindness especially for today, when there is so much hunger for God.

I am pleased to be among you, and there is only one reason why I have traveled here: that all of us may try to be genuine co-workers of Jesus. As you know, a Missionary of Charity is a messenger of God's love.

My impression is that, with time, each one of us will become a messenger of God's love. In order to attain that, we have to go deeper in our life of love, of prayer, of sacrifice. It is very difficult to give Jesus to others if we do not have him first in our hearts.

At the Annunciation God made a gift of his Son to Our Lady. And at the very moment that Mary received Jesus she ran out to offer him to others.

The same should happen to each one of us if we want to become real co-workers of Christ: we ought to receive Jesus, we ought to welcome his love and kindness, and we ought to feel a real urgency to offer that to others.

If we have no concern for that, we are wasting our time. Merely working is not enough, but it is enough to carry peace, love, and kindness to today's world. And for that we need no machine-guns or bombs.

We need a deep love and a deep union with Christ in order to be able to give Christ to others. Kindness and love must grow from within and from our union with Christ. A co-worker is nothing but Christ's life shining in today's world.

But before we are able to live that life outside, we must live it in our own homes. Charity begins at home. That is why our first effort should be to make our home into a new Nazareth, where love and peace reign. This can only be accomplished when the family stays together and prays together.

The suffering of today's world is very great. I feel that much restlessness and suffering start with the family. The family today is becoming less united, is not praying together, is not sharing happiness, is beginning to fall apart.

You, our co-workers, have a magnificent opportunity together in the mission of living that life of love, peace, and unity. Through that life you can proclaim to all the winds that Christ is alive.

As you well know, co-workers are dispersed throughout the world. There are about eighty thousand of them; some of them are well-known, others live in anonymity.

I do not wish to have the co-workers become an

organization, not even a welfare or fundraising organization. That is why we must grow in understanding what it means to be a co-worker.

The co-worker has a mission, a mission that can only come from his union with God. From that union with God there flows, as a natural and spontaneous fruit, love of neighbor, love of the poor.

As I said at the Eucharistic Congress in Philadelphia, Jesus becomes the bread of life in order to meet our hunger for God, our hunger for God's love. At the same time, in order to satisfy his hunger for our love, he has become hungry, naked, homeless. And he has said, "As often as you did it for one of my least brothers, you did it for me" (Mt 25:40).

That is why I say that the Missionaries of Charity and the co-workers should live our lives to the fullest. We are contemplatives in the midst of the world because we touch Christ twenty-four hours a day. Our eucharistic union with Christ should bear that fruit, since Jesus has said, "I am the vine, you are the branches" (John 15:5). Grapes are in the branches, not on the stalk. How great then is your responsibility and mine, the responsibility of us all, since the fruit will depend on the union of the branches to the vine!

Hence our union with Christ must be something real, not mere fantasy. It must be alive, deeply felt, the fruit of conviction. And it must bear fruit first of all in the family. If we do not love our family from within, and if we do not love our neighbor, then our life is a failure.

Christ has chosen you so that you will be able to live out precisely this great vocation: your loving vocation as co-workers. Why you and not others? Why me and not others? I do not know; it is a mystery. But being together should help us to deepen our knowledge of God, and that knowledge will lead us to love him, and love will lead us to serve him.

When you or I attempt to discover Christ's face in

others, Jesus cannot deceive us. It was he who said, "I was hungry, I was naked, I was homeless . . ." (See Mt. 25:31-46). And yet, above all our duty is to care for our own children, for our own families, then for others.

There is much, much suffering in the world. The material suffering is the pain of hunger, of exile, of all kinds of misfortune. However, I believe that the greatest suffering is to feel alone, unwanted, unloved. It is the suffering of not having anyone, of having forgotten what human contact is, what human love is, what it means to be wanted, to be loved, to belong to some human group.

This can occur even in rich families. And that is why I stress our duty to carry out our mission of love to our families above all.

Several weeks ago, in the United States, we held a meeting of co-workers very similar to this one. I was very pleased with it. It helped us to deepen our love of God and of our neighbor.

Everyone left the meeting with a better knowledge of the mission that has been entrusted to each one in the life of Christ in the world, in order to give Christ to others. I felt inwardly enriched, and it seems to me that I received much more from the co-workers than I was able to give them. I believe the same will happen on this occasion.

Now I want to give you some news about the Missionaries of Charity.

Houses have been opened in Mexico and in Guatemala. In Mexico it was the President himself who asked the sisters to come.

On June 25, the feast of the Sacred Heart, we established a contemplative branch of the Missionaries of Charity in New York. We already have seven postulants there. These sisters will live out the word of God in adoration and contemplation, in silence and penitence. For about two hours each day they will proclaim the word of God to the people, not in large groups but on an individual basis.

I am convinced that this work will obtain for us many graces from heaven, for each and every one of us. It will represent a new strength, a new joy. The contemplatives who are united to us in a spiritual bond have become new vigor for the Missionaries of Charity. A powerful force is developing in the world through this sharing together, praying together, suffering together, and working together.

One thing I would like to insist on is that we invest all our effort to ensure that our work for the poor be a work of love. In order to keep it like that it must be built on sacrifice.

As you well know, our sisters commit themselves wholeheartedly to the free service of the poorest poor, and through this vow we put all of our trust in divine providence. Co-workers do not accept any kind of recompense for their work, nor do we make up a fundraising organization.

I have been in many countries and have had the opportunity to address countless people. I say everywhere that I am not looking for money, that I want nothing that flows from abundance: I only ask people to give to the point of hurting. We have to carry out God's work with love and sacrifice.

We have to make it clear that all the money, food, medicine, or whatever people give to the co-workers or to the Missionaries of Charity is used exclusively for the poor we serve. It is true that there are poor everywhere, but when somebody gives you something because you are a co-worker or when you raise money, this is to be used *only* to benefit those poor who are in touch with the Missionaries or the Missionary Brothers of Charity.

This constitutes an act of justice toward the poor in

whose name we accept such gifts. It is also a matter of courtesy, both toward the poor and toward those who have given you their money. They expect all that you collect—up to the last penny, up to the last bottle of medicine, up to the last piece of clothing—to reach the poor of Mother Teresa and the Missionaries of Charity.

The donor's intention deserves our greatest consideration. No co-worker has the right to decide to whom he will assign the money he has received. If the donor has given it for the poor—for the orphans, for the dying, or for the Missionaries of Charity—the donation must be destined to that end.

It is not possible to receive money from other countries without special permission each time. Do not send money directly to India; instead, refer it to India through the co-workers of your country.

There is something I do not allow in India and would not want you to do: to ask people to commit themselves to give a certain amount of money every week or every month. We rely on divine providence, and I wouldn't want people to get used to the idea that we are looking forward to their offerings, that we desire their money, that we are a group of men, women, and children who are on the lookout for how much money we can get from them. This would be the last thing I would want, and I want it to be the last thing for you too. Let's try not even to give the impression that we are looking for how much we can collect, how much we can expend, how much we have in the bank.

Co-workers too must depend on divine providence and not go astray. If people give, thanks be to God; but do not occupy your time in raising money or in making money. Refrain from doing publicity, from writing letters to ask for money, from making things to sell. I would rather have you use your time in an effective service to the poor.

Let us take a spirit of sacrifice to the lives of our brethren. I think this is what Jesus wants of us, and I will never get tired of repeating it: let us offer all we accomplish to the glory of God, and let us ask him to transform us into instruments of peace, of love, of goodness.

I would like the fifteenth chapter of John to become our life. Jesus said, "I am the vine, you are the branches." Let us, then, be the branches.

The congregation of the Missionaries of Charity is a branch, and all the co-workers are small branches united to the larger one. And all of us are united to Jesus. This is the best image of what we represent for the world.

The "liaisons" in each country are united to the main branch, the Missionaries of Charity, and the Missionaries of Charity are united to Jesus. All of the fruit is in the branches in each country. This is a magnificent image of what all of us, the Missionaries of Charity and the co-workers, should be—closely united. Let us not forget that it is in the branches that one finds the fruit, not anywhere else.

All of you should be united, knowing each other and thus staying united. In that way your presence will be greatly effective in the world you live in. Even though it may not be possible for you to attend meetings and similar events, your unity is necessary. Only a life of unity will bear fruit—first in the family, and then all around you.

Judgment of Love

At the moment of death we will not be judged by the amount of work we have done but by the weight of love we have put into our work. This love should flow from self-sacrifice, and it must be felt to the point of hurting.

Love and Leprosy

The heart of the Missionaries of Charity has been given to the four million lepers in our country. Leprosy is, undoubtedly, a very hard illness, but not as hard as feeling deprived of love, feeling unwanted, or being abandoned. Lepers may seem disfigured, but, as are the poor, all of them are wonderful people, capable of much love.

Spiritual Solidarity

The incurably ill can become very close co-workers to a Missionary of Charity by offering their suffering for that sister or brother. Every sister and brother can thus have a second self to pray and suffer for her or for him.

Everyone will draw from this support a new strength, and their lives will be like the burning lamp that wastes away for the sake of souls.

To Suffering Co-workers

Suffering is nothing by itself, but suffering that is shared with the passion of Christ is a wonderful gift and a sign of love. God is very good to give you so much suffering and so much love. All this becomes for me a real joy, and it gives me great strength because of you.

It is your life of sacrifice that gives me so much strength. Your prayers and suffering are like the chalice in which those of us who work can pour the love of the souls we encounter. So you are just as necessary as we are. We and you together can do all things in him who strengthens us.

How beautiful is your vocation of suffering co-workers: you are messengers of God's love. We carry in our hearts the love of God, who is thirsty for souls; you can quench his thirst through your incomparable suffering, to which our hard work is united. It is you who have tasted the chalice of his agony.

The Gift of Smiling

Without our suffering, our task would be merely a social task, very beautiful and useful but not Jesus' work. It would not be a part of redemption.

Jesus has wished to offer us his help by sharing our life, our loneliness, our agony, our death. It was necessary for him to become one with us in order to save us.

We are allowed to do likewise. The afflictions of the poor, not only their material misery but also their spiritual lowliness, are to be redeemed. We have to share these afflictions, since only by becoming one with the poor will we be able to save them—that is, to bring God into their lives and to bring them to God.

When suffering comes close to us, let us accept it with a smile. This is God's greatest gift: having the courage to accept with a smile all he gives us and all he requires of us.

Sharing with Christ

Sacrifice, in order to be genuine, has to empty us of ourselves.

We often say to Christ, Make us partakers of your suffering. But, when someone is insensitive to us, how easily we forget that this is the moment to share with Christ! It would be enough for us to remember that it is Jesus who gives us, through such a person or circumstance, the opportunity to do something beautiful for him.

Sister, superiors, try to see Christ in your sisters. They belong to him; love them as you love Christ.

Sisters, lift up your eyes to see Christ in your superiors. Your superior is the vine; you are the branch. If you do not allow the vinedresser to prune you, you will not bear fruit.

On September 10 we will celebrate the twenty-fifth anniversary of our congregation. There is no better way to show the deepest gratitude than by accepting one another as you are and renewing your smile every day.

The Heart of the Poor

News from Bangladesh seems to be worse each day. Hatred and selfishness are destroying a whole nation. Right now, when people are tortured and undergoing unheard-of suffering, let us avoid everything that may cause wounds in the heart of the poor.

We have no right to use what belongs to the poor. We are to eat nothing in the house of the rich; thus we will be able to say to the poor who offer us something to drink, "We have not accepted anything from others."

People like to see the sisters accompanied by Mary. With rosary in hand, they are always willing to spread the good news.

The Joy of the Virgin

Let Mary be the cause of our joy. Let each one of us be Jesus to her.

No one learned humility as well as Mary did. She was the slave girl. Being a slave means to be used by all, with joy.

Joy was the Virgin's strength. Only joy could give her the strength to walk without getting tired up to the hill country of Judea in order to carry out a servant's work. We too have to walk without stopping and go beyond the hills of trouble.

Loving and Suffering

Love begins in the family. Do not be afraid to love to the point of hurting.

Love your superiors. The congregation will be what you are with your superior: a fruitful branch or a dry branch.

The Rich for the Poor (and Vice Versa)

There are families of upper castes who adopt children we have picked up in the streets. This is a genuine revolution, given the caste prejudices. When this happens, the rich person becomes better because he shows God's love for the poor; and the poor one becomes better through the love he receives from the rich.

The Poor Are Important

I believe that in today's world the most important person is the one who is poor. He possesses the resources of suffering and of working hard.

The Degree of Love

Do not pursue spectacular deeds. What matters is the gift of your self, the degree of love that you put into each one of your actions.

The Weapon of Love

We need no bombs or weapons. Love is our weapon: love toward the lepers, the elderly, the dying, the paralytic; toward all those who have no one and are loved by no one.

Poverty

God has not created poverty; it is we who have created it. Before God, all of us are poor.

The Church

The church is each one of us: you, I. We are the ones who have to know, love, and put ourselves at the service of the poorest.

The Heart of the Church

If we can realize that we religious sisters are the slave girls of the Lord, just as the Virgin Mary was, then the future of religious life will be holy. We religious sisters are like the heart of our mother the church.

The Fish and Darkness

There is a saying, "Don't give someone a fish, but teach him how to catch a fish."

In India we say that "it is better to light a candle than to curse the darkness."

We attempt to serve the poor every day, and thus to uphold love, the commandment of Christ—working, serving, living closely to the poorest.

Forgiving

When we realize that we are sinners needing forgiveness, it will be very easy for us to forgive others. If I do not understand this, it will be very hard for me to say "I forgive you" to anyone who comes to me.

It is not necessary to be a Christian in order to forgive. Every human being comes from God's hand, and we all know how much God loves us. No matter what our belief is, we have to learn how to forgive if we really want to love.

Humility and Forgiveness

All of us should work for peace. But to obtain that peace all of us have to learn from Jesus to be meek and humble of heart. Only humility will lead us to unity, and unity to peace. To that end, let us help each other draw closer to Jesus, so that we may learn the lesson of humility with joy.

Let us think about oppressed countries. The greatest need of Bangladesh is forgiveness—there is so much bitterness and hatred! It is impossible to imagine how those people suffer. If they realize that we care for them, that we love them, perhaps they will find strength in their hearts to forgive. I think this is the only thing that can bring them peace.

We want this year to be, above all, a year of peace. With that aim, we will try to talk more with God than with men.

Let us spread Christ's peace as he did. He planted good everywhere. He did not forsake his works of charity because the Pharisees and others rejected him and tried to spoil his Father's work.

Cardinal Newman wrote: "Help me, wherever I may be, to spread your perfume. May I preach you without preaching—without words but with my example, through the force of attraction, the example of my actions, the obvious fullness of love that carries my heart to you."

Suffering with Christ

Suffering is nothing by itself. But suffering shared with the passion of Christ is a wonderful gift, the most beautiful gift, a token of love. By giving up his Son, the

Father has given the world a token of his love. It was a gift, the greatest gift of love, for his suffering was his expiation for sin.

The suffering of Bengal is an enormous Calvary, where the body of Christ is again crucified.

Hunger and Luxury

The co-workers acknowledge that all the goods of this world are free gifts of God and that no one has a right to superfluous wealth as long as there are some who are starving. Co-workers try to make up for this serious injustice by sacrificing luxury in their daily lives.

The Generosity of Children

Sometimes the rich seem very willing to share in their own way the unhappiness of others. But it is a pity that they never give to the point of feeling that they are in need.

The present generations, especially children, understand better. There are English children who make sacrifices in order to be able to offer a muffin to our children. There are Danish children who make sacrifices in order to be able to offer others a glass of milk every day. And German children do the same in order to be able to offer the poor some fortified food.

These are concrete ways of teaching love. When these children grow up, they will know what it means to give.

Poverty Saves Us

We have to suffer with Christ. In doing this we will share in the sufferings of the poor.

Our congregation may die if the sisters do not walk in Christ's rhythm in his suffering and if they do not live in poverty. Our rigorous poverty is our safeguard. We do not want, as has been the case with other religious orders throughout history, to begin serving the poor and then gradually move toward serving the rich.

In order for us to understand and to be able to help those who lack everything, we have to live as they live. The difference lies only in the fact that those we aid are poor by force, whereas we are poor by choice.

Helping One Person

The sisters do small things—helping children, visiting those who are isolated, the sick, those who lack everything.

In one of the houses the sisters visit they found a woman who had died alone a few days earlier. Her body had already begun decomposing. The neighbors didn't even know her name.

When someone tells me that what the sisters do is irrelevant, that they limit themselves to things that are little less than ordinary, I reply that even if they helped only one person, that would be reason enough for their work. Jesus would have died for one person, for one sinner.

Not Judging

Who are we to judge the rich? It is our duty to put the poor and the rich face-to-face, to be their point of encounter.

Life Belongs to God

I think that the cry of children who are assassinated before they come into the world is surely heard by God.

Jesus has said that we are much more important in the eyes of his Father than the grass, the birds, or the lilies of the field. He has also said that if the Father cares for all these things, much more will he care for his own life in us.

Jesus cannot deceive us. Life is the greatest gift of God to human beings, and man has been created in the image of God. Life belongs to God, and we have no right to destroy it.

Giving and Self-Giving

I would like co-workers to put their hands and their hearts at the service of others. If they do not make contact with the poor, they will not be able to know who they are.

Here in Calcutta we have a number of non-Christians and Christians who work together in the House of the Dying and other places. There are also some who offer their care to the lepers.

One day an Australian man came and made a substantial donation. But as he did this he said, "This is something external. Now I want to give something of myself." He now comes regularly to the House of the Dying to shave the sick men and to converse with them.

This man gives not only his money but also his time. He could have spent it on himself, but what he wants is to give himself.

Co-workers of Christ

We should love our congregation and be thankful for all that God and society expect of us: they expect us to be genuine co-workers of Christ. More than ever, let us accomplish our task for the poor with a humble and generous heart.

The Flame of Love

In order to survive, love must feed on sacrifice. Jesus' words, "Love each other as I have loved you," should not only be a light for us but also a flame to burn away our selfishness. Loving should be just as natural as living and breathing.

St. Therese of Lisieux used to say, "When I act and think with charity, I feel that it is Jesus who works in me. The deeper my union with him, the stronger is my love for those who live in Carmel."

Christ's Instruments

We put our hands, our eyes, and our hearts at Christ's disposal, so that he will act through us.

Kindness and Understanding

We will never know all the good a simple smile can do.

We speak about our God who is good, merciful, and compassionate. Are we a living token of that reality? Those who suffer—can they perceive in us that goodness, that forgiveness, that living understanding?

May no one ever come to you without going away better and happier. Everyone should see kindness in your face, in your eyes, in your smile.

Thinking about Others

In the poor neighborhoods we are God's light and kindness.

Foresight is the beginning of holiness. If you learn this art of foreseeing, you will be more and more like Christ, for his heart was sweet and he would always think about others.

Our vocation, in order to be beautiful, should be full of attention toward others. Jesus went about doing good everywhere. At Cana Our Lady did nothing but think about the needs of others and report them to Jesus.

Love for the Person

It is the individual that is important to us. In order to love a person, one must come close to him or her. If we wait until there is a given number of people, we will get lost in numbers and will never be able to show respect and love for one concrete person.

To me, every person in the world is unique.

Dignity of the Poor

I believe that the men of today think that the poor are not humanly similar to them. They look down upon them. I am convinced that if they had a deep respect for the poor, it would be easier for them to get close to the poor and to see that they are as much entitled to the things of life and to love as any other human being.

In these times of development, the whole world runs and is hurried. But there are some who fall down on the way and have no strength to go ahead. These are the ones we should care about.

I never look at the crowds, but at one person. If I looked at the crowds, I would never begin.

Love is a fruit in season at all times.

In the Slums

Our sisters work in the slums. There we frequently run across young mothers who are about to die and children with deformities. Through research we discovered that men have abused these young women, taking advantage of their ignorance.

We began to ask God to send us someone to take care of this work, to help such women cope with this difficulty with a clear conscience, a healthy body, and in a happy family. There came to us a sister from Mauritius Island who had attended a course on family planning.

We started with an information program. Right now there are more than three thousand families who use natural family planning, and it has been about 95 percent effective. When people see these good effects in their families, they come to us to say thanks. Some of them have said, "Our family has stayed together, in good health, and we can have a child when we desire it."

The Human Promotion of the Poor

We have no right to judge the rich. For our part, what we desire is not a class struggle but a class encounter, in which the rich save the poor and the poor save the rich.

We favor making the poor responsible. We ask their collaboration; we invite them to look for solutions themselves.

In Calcutta there are poor people who survive by serving in the houses of those who have more. They even come to offer their work *gratis* to our centers. Perhaps for just a half-hour each week. This is a way of putting themselves at the level of the rest of men.

Christ in the Poor

I often ask for gifts that have nothing to do with money. There are things one can get. What I desire is the presence of the donor, for him to touch those to whom he gives, for him to smile at them, for him to pay attention to them. All of this is very meaningful for those people.

Jesus met Saul while he was hurrying to Damascus to create agitation, to kill and to do away with Christians. Jesus said to him, "Saul, Saul, why do you persecute me?"

Saul answered, "Who are you, sir?"

Jesus said, "I am Jesus, the one you are persecuting."

Today it is the same Christ, the same Jesus, who identifies with the poor whom we consider undesirable. They are useless for society, and no one has any time to devote to them. It is you and I, if our love is genuine, who are to discover them.

Commitment to the Poor

With no opportunity to receive the religious message, the most upright and intelligent spirit is in fact nothing but a bee locked up in a bottle.

I urge people to join our work for our profit and for the profit of everyone. I never ask them for money or any material thing. I ask them to bring their love, to offer the sacrifice of their hands.

When these people run across those in need, their first move is to do something. When they come the second time, they already feel committed. After some time they feel they belong to the poor and that they are filled with the need to love. They discover who they are and what it is that they themselves can give.

Admirable Lepers

In Calcutta we have picked up thousands of lepers. I assure you, they are admirable, no matter how disfigured they appear in our sight.

The Little Orphan's Appetite

In order for love to be genuine, it has to reach first of all those who are closest to us. It is this love that brings us to God.

Our sisters and brothers, as well as our co-workers, try to live out this love of God by means of love of their neighbors. Only knowledge of the poor will lead them to serve.

Those who helped us during the difficulties that the Bengali refugees underwent claimed that they had received more from those they helped than they had been able to give. This is exactly what each one of us experiences when we come in touch with the poorest poor.

This is what our people need: they need our hands to serve them and our hearts to offer them love.

Think about the loneliness of the elderly: without resources, without love, with no one to aid them. Think about abandoned children. In many places we become aware of this suffering, of this hunger for love that only you and I can meet.

One day I discovered a poor child who would not eat. His mother was dead. I found a sister who looked very much like his mother. I told her to do nothing but take care of the child. His appetite returned.

The Light of Christ

Every sister and brother ought to grow in the likeness of Christ so that Christ may live his life of compassion and humility in today's world.

How great your love for Christ is! Keep the light of Christ always shining in your hearts. He is the love that must be loved.

Spreading God's Love

Love is a fruit in season and out of season, without limits—a fruit that is available to all.

Are we convinced of Christ's love for us and of our love for him? Is this conviction a sunbeam that increases the sap of life and makes petals of holiness bud? Is this conviction the rock on which holiness is built, in the service of the poor, delivering to them what we would like to offer to Christ himself?

If we follow this path, our faith will grow; and through

our growing conviction, the pursuit of holiness will become our daily task.

God loves those to whom he can give more, those who expect more from him, those who are open, those who sense their need and rely on him for everything. Our works are just an expression of the growth of God's love in us. Therefore, he who is more united to God is the one who loves his neighbor more.

May the love of Christ be a living bond between every two of us. From that others will realize that we are true Missionaries of Charity.

It may happen that a mere smile, a short visit, the lighting of a lamp, writing a letter for a blind man, carrying a bucket of charcoal, offering a pair of sandals, reading the newspaper for someone—something small, very small—may, in fact, be our love of God in action.

Even if this year we should collect less money, much less, the important thing is that we continue to spread Christ's love. If we give Christ to him who is hungry—not only for bread but also for our love, for our presence, for our contact—then this year could well be the year of the real live explosion of the love that God brings to our earth.

Without God we can spread only pain and suffering around us.

Co-workers of Christ

On listening to the call of the poor, co-workers are to have a special care for those who feel unwanted and deprived of love. The worst illness today is not leprosy or tuberculosis but the sense of being unwanted, of not being loved, of being abandoned by all.

The greatest sin is the absence of love or charity—the terrible indifference toward the neighbor who, right on the street, falls victim to exploitation, to corruption, to starving, and to sickness.

Every co-worker, destined as he is to cooperate with Christ in the work of mercy, must understand what God and society expect of him: that the poor, as they see the co-worker, may feel drawn toward Christ and invite Christ to enter their lives; that the sick and all those who suffer may find in him a true angel of consolation; that, as he walks the street, the children may come to him because he reminds them of him who proclaimed himself the friend of children.

Mutual Concern

If we learn the art of recollection, we will look more and more like Christ since his heart is nothing but reward: Christ always thinks about others.

Jesus walked among men doing only good. At Cana Mary did nothing but think about the needs of others and let Jesus know about them.

The recollection of Jesus, Mary, and Joseph was so deep that they changed Nazareth into the dwelling of the Almighty. If we too could have that same concern for one another, our communities would also become the dwelling places of the Almighty.

The Power of Joy

Joy is strength. The poor felt attracted to Jesus because a higher power dwelt in him and flowed from him—out of his eyes, his hands, his body—completely released and present to God and to men.

Prayer and Work

Christ will not ask us how many things we have done but how much love we have put into our actions.

The poor are a gift from God: they are our love. There are many who are spiritually poor. The spiritual poverty that one finds in Europe and in America is a difficult burden to carry. It is very difficult to take the love of God as a witness to those countries.

Our spiritual life is a life of reliance on God. It's fruit is the work for the poor. Our work is our prayer because we carry it out through Jesus, in Jesus, and for the sake of Jesus.

The Poor

The poor are a hope. They represent, in fact, the hope of the world through their courage. They offer us a different way of loving God, by urging us to do all we can to help them.

Dear Sisters

God needs our poverty, not our abundance.
The means of being humble:
- speak as little as possible about oneself
- take care of one's personal matters
- avoid curiosity
- do not meddle in the affairs of others
- accept contradictions with good humor
- do not focus on the faults of others
- accept reproach, even if undeserved
- yield to the will of others
- accept insults and abuse
- accept feeling uncared for, forgotten, despised
- be courteous and sensitive, even if someone provokes you
- do not try to be admired and loved
- do not hide behind one's own dignity
- yield in arguments, even if one is right
- always choose what is most difficult.

The Joy of the Poor

Strive to be the demonstration of God in the midst of your community. We have to radiate the joy of being poor, with no need for words. We must be happy in our poverty.

Let Us Submit to Christ

I am going across the ocean once more in order to show you how to look for the poor.

Dom Marmion wrote: "All you have to do is abandon yourselves in his hands like wax, so that he will cut without fear the useless parts." For his part, when Dom Marmion underwent the temptation to abandon his order, he prostrated himself in front of the tabernacle and shouted out, "May I be broken into pieces rather than abandon the monastery!"

Are we strong enough, to the point of preferring to be cut into pieces rather than abandon Christ? One cannot change one's profession as easily as one can change dress.

In our day all things grow weaker. Even the most sacred ties are untied. Let us submit to the Rock, who is Christ.

Love and Renewal

To work without love is slavery.

The church wants renewal, but renewal does not mean changing customs. Renewal must be faithful to the spirit of the texts.

Brides of Christ

Offer to God all your words, your actions. We are to be brides of Christ. Let it never be said that there is a woman in this world who loves her husband more than we love Christ.

The Silence of the Heart

I like to recommend silence. The silence of the tongue will teach us to talk to Christ; the silence of the eyes will help us see God.

Our eyes resemble two windows through which either Christ or the world can come in. Sometimes we need courage to keep them closed.

Let us keep the silence of the heart, just as did the Virgin, who kept everything in her heart.

Faithfulness

We who are espoused to Christ cannot make room for other affections in our heart without provoking God's discontent. God has chosen us, but he also has a right to stop choosing us. He will never do that unless we force him to do so. Do not play with your vocation because when you want to preserve it you will lack the courage to do it.

Why so many broken homes? Because of uncontrolled affections, because of the desire to have all the pleasures that come from two loves.

When we left everything to enter religious life, our parents made great sacrifices. If we are unfaithful to our vocation, we will cause them a very deep affliction.

The Vow of Charity

The vow of charity is a fruit of our union with Christ, just as a child is the fruit of the sacrament of matrimony. Just as a lamp cannot burn without oil, so also a vow of charity cannot live without the vows of poverty and obedience.

Nazareth

Mary's foresight was so great that she made Nazareth into a shelter for God.

Use your tongue for the good of others—for out of the abundance of the heart the mouth speaks.

Smiles of Joy

Novices, I desire to hear the music of your smiles of joy.
Young professed sisters, the noise of your steps in search of souls must be a sweet music for Jesus.

Students, the lamp that burns over your books you must provide with a good supply of oil so that you will be able to be a light of Christ in the slums.

Prayers for the Pope

Yesterday we went to St. Peter's ica, where a public audience was held. Afterward the Pope received us in a private audience. There were forty of us.

I don't remember a single word. I only know that he asked for prayers. None of us remember anything else because all we did was look at him.

The Dust of our Souls

This year we ought to prepare a manger of poverty. It will be easy to fill it up with charity.

We are convinced that we know each other very well personally. Our lives belong to God—why spend so much time analyzing ourselves?

The problem is not that we don't make our examination of conscience but that we do it by ourselves. We must do it with Christ if it is to be a sincere examination—Jesus is our "co-worker."

Our souls should be like a transparent crystal through which God can be perceived. This crystal is sometimes covered with dirt and dust. To remove this dust we carry out our examination of conscience, in order to obtain a clean heart.

God will help us to remove that dust, as long as we allow him to, if our will is that his will come about. Perhaps this is what we have lacked.

Our duties, our attitude toward our neighbor, our contacts, can offer us matter for reflection. If we carry out our examination without anything to divert our attention, we will realize that we need Jesus to help us discover our unfaithfulnesses.

Our examination of conscience is the mirror we focus toward nature: a human test, no doubt, but one that needs a mirror in order to faithfully reflect its faults. If we undertake this task with greater faithfulness, perhaps we will realize that what we sometimes consider a stumbling block is rather a rock we can step on.

Humility

The more visible our life, the more we need humility. It is beautiful to see the humility of Christ, who *emptied* himself and took the form of a slave.

People surround us with their love in order to ensure the usefulness of our work.

People do not like religious sisters who are arrogant because they are a heavy instrument in the hands of God. The poor should be treated as children of God, not as slaves. It is a great virtue to practice humility without knowing that you are humble.

Christ

There is only one strong prayer: Christ. There is only one voice that rises over the face of the earth: the voice of Christ.

Humility and the Gifts of God

It is said that humility is the truth and that Jesus is the truth. Consequently, the only way to be like Christ is to practice humility.

But let us not think that humility is shown by hiding

God's gifts. We have to use all the gifts that God has
bestowed on us.

Obedience and Reward

On December 31, while the sirens were welcoming the
new year, my thoughts were with each one of you.

Let us be apostles of obedience who spread Jesus' joy in
the house we are in. God loves you through your
superiors, whom he has put over you in place of himself.
If he rewards even for a glass of water, how much more
will he reward your expenses of obedience!

Seeking Jesus

St. Margaret Mary once asked Jesus, "Lord, what do
you want me to do?"

Jesus replied, "Let *me* work."

Let yourselves be emptied and transformed in order to
fill the cup of your heart to its fullest. Then you in turn
will be able to give in abundance.

Seek him; knowledge will make you strong as death.
Love him without looking back, without fear. Believe that
only Jesus is life. Serve him, rejecting and forgetting
whatever may hinder you, with the sole desire that the
love which is not loved be loved.

Learning from the Virgin

May the Virgin make our hearts humble and sub-
missive like her son's heart. In her the heart of Jesus was
formed.

Let us learn to be humble, accepting humiliations with
joy. We have been created for great things—why then
should we stoop to things that would blur the beauty of
our heart?

How many things we can learn from the Virgin! Ask

the Virgin to tell Jesus, "They have no more wine"—the wine of humility and submission, of goodness, of sweetness.

Obeying as Christ

The first lesson of the heart of Jesus is our examination of conscience: know thyself. The examination consists of facing ourselves with Jesus. We should not waste time looking at our misery, but we are rather to look in to his light.

In our vow of obedience, don't we lack faith if we stop to look at the human limitations of our superiors? Our prompt, simple, and joyous obedience is the best demonstration of our faith.

If God loves him who gives joyfully, how much more will he love him who gives with obedience! To obey as Christ has obeyed.

Humility of Heart

Mary's greatness lay in her humility. It is not surprising that Jesus, who lived so close to her, seems determined to have us learn one thing above all: humility of heart.

Humility is truth. We must be able to say with Paul, "In him who is the source of my strength I have strength for everything" (Phil 4:13).

By yourselves you can get nothing but weakness, misery, and sin. All the gifts you have come from God. Do not allow temptations to weaken the strength of your vocation.

Obeying

In heaven our Lord will not ask you, "Was your superior intelligent, understanding, cheerful?" He will simply ask you, "Have you obeyed me?"

What a failure your life will be if it is only full of yourself instead of being full of him, who is our bridegroom!

If you are not able to see Jesus in your superior, how will you see him in the poor? How will you discover Jesus under the appearance of misery? How will you love Jesus whom you cannot see, if you do not love your superior whom you see?

When the devil is discontented with God's work and does not know how to destroy it, he tries to destroy the instrument. And in that way, indirectly, he destroys God's work.

Do not let yourselves be taken advantage of. Obey obey—no matter whom or what, since the superior represents God.

Obey just as the Virgin obeyed the angel: "Let it be done to me as you say" (Lk 1:38). As who said? As the angel himself said, for the angel was in God's place. She the queen of heaven, obeyed an angel—just as she obeyed St. Joseph, who was in God's place for her.

The Oil and the Lamp

Do not think that love, in order to be genuine, has to be extraordinary. What we need is to love without getting tired.

How does a lamp burn? Through the continuous input of small drops of oil. If the drops of oil run out, the light of the lamp will cease, and the bridegroom will say, "I do not know you" (see Mt 25:1-13).

My daughters, what are these drops of oil in our lamps? They are the small things of daily life: faithfulness, punctuality, small words of kindness, a thought for others, our way of being silent, of looking, of speaking, and of acting. These are the true drops of love that keep your religious life burning like a lively flame.

Do not look for Jesus away from yourselves. He is no

out there; he is in you. Keep your lamp burning, and you will recognize him.

The Suffering of the Poor

Without suffering, our work would merely be a social work—charitable and healthy, but not Jesus' work. Christ has wanted to share our life, our loneliness, our anguish, our death. All of that, during the hardest night ever. . .

All the unhappiness of the poor—their material poverty, their spiritual abandonment—may be redeemed if we share their suffering. Only by remaining united with them will we be able to save them.

Obedience and Holiness

How great your vocation is! How happy would many be if they were offered the opportunity to serve personally the king of the world! Well, that is what we are doing. We can touch, serve, and love Christ every day of our lives.

Your work on behalf of the poor will be better carried out if you know how God wants you to carry it out, but you will have no way of knowing that, other than by obedience. Submit to your superiors, just like ivy. Ivy cannot live if it does not hold fast to something; you will not grow or live in holiness unless you hold fast to obedience.

Great Things and Small Things

Be faithful in small things because it is in them that your strength lies. Nothing is small for our good God, for he is great and we are small. That is why he lowers himself and cares to do small things, in order to offer us an opportunity to show him our love. Since he does them, they are great things, they are infinite. Nothing he does can be small.

I will take all of you with me up to the feet of the Vicar of Christ. I am sure that he will bless each one of you with his fatherly love.

Faithfulness to the Rule

Faithfulness to the rule is the most delicate and precious flower we can offer God. The rule expresses God's will: we have to submit to it to our last breath.

When the rule becomes one of the things we love most, that love becomes a free service that is carried out with a smile. Submission, for a person who loves, is more than a duty; it is the secret of holiness.

We are to be persuaded that even the smallest unjustified transgression wounds the heart of Jesus and stains our conscience. We must be faithful in small things, not for themselves—for that would be for petty spirits—but because of God's will, which we always have to respect in small things.

St. Augustine used to say, "Small things are really small, but being faithful in small things is a great thing."

Our Lord—isn't he the same Lord in a small host or in a large one? The smallest rule contains God's will, no less than the great things of life.

In order to understand this truth, we must be convinced that the rule has a divine origin. We must hold fast to it, as a small child holds fast to his mother.

We must love this truth with our will and with our reason. It does not matter if sometimes it seems hard, austere, and artificial. God has been so wonderful to us; it is our duty to be wonderful toward him.

Love for the Rule

All of us have to carry out something beautiful for God. We are able to imagine all sorts of mortifications. Only one thing counts: living out the rule with the greatest love.

St. Vincent compares the rules with "wings for flying toward God."

On her deathbed a religious sister asked, "What would I have had to do in order to be a saint?" The priest who was assisting her answered, "Do you not know this wonderful book which is the rule? If you had lived it out, you would be a saint."

"It should be enough for you to know that by fulfilling your duties you will be saints," says St. Alphonsus.

St. Vincent says, "Observe your rules and you will be saints because since the rule is holy it will make you holy."

St. Francis de Sales writes, "Go forth always faithfully observing your rule, and you will be blessed by God since he himself will guide you with all care."

In the observance of the rule you will find strength for the purity of your conscience, fervor to fill your soul, and love to inflame your heart.

Smiling at Jesus

Do not be blind, my daughters. The good God has delivered his work to you; you must carry it out the way he wants. Success and failure have no meaning whatsoever before him, as long as you do what he is asking of you and in the way he is asking it of you. If you obey, you will be infallible.

The devil attempts everything in order to destroy God's work. But since he cannot obtain that directly, he tries to make us carry out God's work our own way. It is right there that he wins and we lose.

In all our houses and in the novitiate God grants generosity to the religious sisters. Preserve that generosity—you will have all reason to feel happy. Continue smiling at Jesus, through a smile at your superiors, at your sisters, at the poor.

We have to make all effort to do good. "I want it," said St. John Berchmans, St. Stanislaus, St. Margaret Mary, and they became saints.

What is a saint? He or she is a resolved soul, a soul who uses his own strength in order to work. This is what St Paul meant when he asserted, "In him who is the source of my strength I have strength for everything."

Being Holy

My sisters, I would not be satisfied with only seeing that you are good religious sisters. You must be capable of a perfect sacrifice. Only holiness can perfect your commitment.

It is very difficult to resolve to be holy. The soul that has made such a decision is exposed to renunciation, to temptation, to struggle, to persecution, to all sorts of sacrifice.

One cannot love God except at one's own expense.

The words *I want to be holy* mean: I will divest myself of everything that is not of God; I will divest myself and empty my heart of material things; I will live in poverty and in privation; I will renounce my own will, my inclinations, my whims, my fickleness; and I will become a generous slave girl to God's will.

I'm Going on a Trip

I will soon fly to the United States, but my heart and my spirit are staying with you. This is God's will. Therefore you should feel happy.

During my absence our general assistant and the general council will take full responsibility. God will not cease caring for you if you remain together. Remain closely united to the community because God is its center.

I am not worried about leaving you because I know the great gift that God has given me on giving you to me.

During my trip back I will go to Rome. I will try to see the Holy Father, and I will ask him to grant us a pontifical acknowledgment. We do not deserve such a gift, but if it is God's holy will, we will surely get it.

Let the superior make sacrifices in obedience, the sisters in charity, the novices in poverty, and the postulants in chastity.

Superiors, strive for quick, simple, blind, cheerful obedience, for Jesus was obedient unto death.

Sisters, strive for charity in desires, in words, in thoughts, in feelings, in actions, for Jesus went about doing good.

Novices, strive for poverty in desires, in attachments, in tastes and distastes, for Jesus, rich as he was, became poor for our sake.

Postulants, strive for chastity in thoughts, affections, and desires, not listening to useless talk, for God is a jealous husband.

Love of Poverty

I think that if today there are no vocations in the church, or if they are scarce, it is partly due to the fact that there is too much wealth, too much comfort, too high a standard of living, not only in families but even in religious life.

From all parts of the world young people are coming to India to take on a very poor life, poorer than ours. They are driven by the desire to be free from their environment of wealth. I think they want to be a living example of Christ's poverty.

It is not enough to know the spirit of poverty; you have to know poverty itself. Poverty means not having anything. Today everyone, even those who come from well-do-do environments, want to know what it really means to have nothing.

Most of the vocations we receive come from Europe and America. They have asked to join the congregation not because of the work but because of a love for poverty.

Charity and Obedience

On October 7 we will celebrate the anniversary of the day when God wanted our small congregation to come into existence. Since this is a day consecrated to Our Lady, it was only fair that she would grant that we survive up to this wonderful day. Let us strive to be sources of joy in her honor, as she is for us.

We have to grow like straight and fruitful trees. I have in my heart many things to tell you, but there are mainly two: charity and obedience.

Be genuine collaborators of Christ. Shine out his life and live it. Be comforting angels to the sick and friends to the humble.

Love each other as God loves each one of you, with an intense and particular love. Be kind to each other: it is better to commit faults with gentleness than to work miracles with unkindness.

Be moderate in your words. Admire the discretion of the Virgin. She does not miss a single word of the angel's message, but keeps everything in her heart and lets God intervene.

Stand out by your obedience. Help your superiors through a simple, blind, concerned, and cheerful obedience. You may be better endowed, more capable, and even holier than your superior. But only one thing counts: she represents God for you.

Pain and Work

My thoughts often run to you who suffer, and I offer your sufferings which are so great while mine are so small.

Those of you who are sick, when things are hard, take refuge in Christ's heart. There my own heart will find with you strength and love.

Do you desire to suffer with a pure love? Do it with the love that Christ has chosen for you. Give more and more, until you have given everything.

How grateful I am that God has given you to me! My soul is encouraged by the thought that you are offering your prayers and pains for our work's sake. This makes my smile come more easily.

You suffer, we work. You and we together are offering the same chalice.

Discretion and Love

Riches, both material and spiritual, can choke you if you do not use them fairly. Let us remain as empty as possible so that God can fill us up. For not even God can put anything in a heart that is already full. God does not impose himself on us.

It is you, sisters, who can fill the world with the love that God has given you. The work of moral rearmament is carried out with discretion and love. The more discreet, the more penetrating it will be. You give it to others, and it is they who absorb it.

People do not seem very willing to see us, but all of them hunger and thirst for what God wants to give them through us. All over the world men are hungry and thirsty for God's love. You meet that hunger by spreading joy. We show forth our joy in the service of the sick, the dying, and the abandoned.

Smiling

In order to spread joy, joy needs to reign in the family. Peace and war start within one's own home. If we really want peace for the world, let us start by loving one another within our families. We will thus have Christ's joy, which is our strength.

Sometimes it is hard for us to smile at one another. It is often difficult for the husband to smile at his wife or for the wife to smile at her husband. It is sometimes difficult for me to smile at Christ.

Giving Cheerfully

God loves a cheerful giver. He who gives cheerfully gives better.

The best way to show our gratitude to God and to our neighbor is to accept their gifts with joy. Joy is a net of love in which souls can be caught. Joy can multiply itself in a heart that overflows with love.

We impatiently await God's paradise, but we have in our hands the power to be in paradise right here and now. Being happy with God means this: to love as he loves, to help as he helps, to give as he gives, to serve as he serves.

Love in Action

Since we cannot see Christ, we cannot express our love to him. But we do see our neighbor, and we can do for him what we would do for Christ if he were visible.

Let us be open to God, so that he can use us. Let us put love into action.

Let us begin with our family, with our closest neighbors. It is difficult, but that is where our work begins. We are collaborators of Christ, fertile branches on the vine.

The Visible Christ

Both you and we are carrying out the same social work, but whereas some people do it for the sake of something, we do it for the sake of someone. It is here that respect, love, and devotion come into play, since we do it for God's sake, and therefore we want it to be as beautiful as possible.

We are in continuous touch with Christ in his work, just as we are in touch with him at mass and in the Eucharist. There Jesus offers himself under the appearance of bread. In the world of suffering, in damaged bodies, in children, we see Christ and touch him every day.

Knowing the Poor Better

The tabernacle is the guarantee that Jesus has set his tent among us. The Eucharist is the sacrament of prayer, the fountain and summit of Christian life.

Our Eucharist is incomplete if it does not lead us to service and love for the poor. As we receive the communion of the poor, we discover our own poverty.

Every day we sisters have the exposition of the Blessed Sacrament. This has brought a deep change in our lives: we have discovered a deeper love of Christ through the afflicted face of the poor. We have been able to know each other better and to know the poor better too, as a concrete witness of God.

Since we have started this form of worship, we have not diminished our work. We continue to devote to it as much time as before, but with a better understanding. People now accept us better because they are hungry for God. They feel a need not for us but for Jesus.

Holiness Means Wanting

Holiness consists of carrying out God's will with joy. Faithfulness forges saints.

Spiritual life is union with Jesus—the divine and the human in mutual giving. The only thing Jesus asks is that I commit myself to him, in total poverty, in total forgetfulness of self.

The first step toward holiness is the will to attain it. With a will that is whole we love God, we opt for him, we run toward him, we reach him, we possess him. Often, under the pretext of humility, of confidence, of abandonment, we forget about using our will. But it all depends on these words—*I want* or *I do not want*. I have to pour all of my energy into the words *I want*.

We cannot decide to become saints without a great effort of renunciation, of resisting temptations, of combat, of persecution, and of all sorts of sacrifices. It is not possible to love God except at one's own expense.

The Poor Are Our Prayer

We begin our day by trying to see Christ through the eucharistic bread. Throughout the day we keep in touch with him under the appearances of the shattered bodies of our poor. In this way our work becomes a prayer, as we accomplish it with Jesus, for Jesus, and toward Jesus.

The poor are our prayer. They carry God in themselves. Prayer is in all things, in all gestures.

Prayer and Silence

It is difficult to pray if you don't know how to do it. We need to help each other in prayer.

Silence is the most important element. Souls of prayer are souls of deep silence. We cannot place ourselves directly in the presence of God without forcing ourselves to an inner and an outer silence. Therefore, we have to get used to the silence of the spirit, of the eyes, and of the tongue.

God is a friend of silence. We cannot find him in noise or agitation. Nature—trees, flowers, grass—grows in silence. The stars, the moon, and the sun move in silence.

Is it not our mission to give God to the poor of the street? Not a dead God but a living God, a God of love.

The apostles say, "We have to concentrate on prayer and the ministry of the word" (see Acts 6:4). The more we receive in our silent prayer, the more we will be able to give in our active life. Silence gives us a new vision of things. We need that silence in order to get through to souls. What is essential is not what we say but what God tells us and what he tells others through us.

Jesus always waits for us in silence. In silence he listens to us; in silence he speaks to our souls. In silence we are granted the privilege of listening to his voice.

Interior silence is very difficult; we have to make efforts to pray. In that silence we will discover a new energy and a real unity—the unity of our thoughts with his, the unity of our prayers with his, the unity of our actions with his, the unity of our life with his.

All of our words will be useless unless they come from the bottom of our hearts. Words that do not spread the light of Christ increase the darkness.

Overflowing with Joy

What would our life be like if the sisters were not cheerful? It would be mere slavery. We would work without attracting anybody. Sadness, discouragement and slowness open the doors for sloth, which is the mother of all evils.

If you are joyful, do not worry about lukewarmness. Joy will shine in your eyes and in your look, in your conversation and in your countenance. You will not be able to hide it because joy overflows. When people see happiness in your eyes, they will become aware of their nature as children of God.

Holy souls sometimes undergo great inward trial, and they know darkness. But if we want others to become aware of the presence of Jesus, we must be the first ones convinced of it.

Imagine a sister who goes to the slums with a sad face and a slow pace. What can her presence convey to poor people? Nothing but a deeper discouragement.

Joy is very contagious. Try, therefore, to be always overflowing with joy whenever you go among the poor.

Joy, according to St. Bonaventure, has been given to man so that he can rejoice in God because of the hope of the eternal good and on the sight of all the benefits he receives from God. Thus he will know how to rejoice at his neighbor's prosperity, how to be pleased in giving glory to God, and how to feel discontent concerning empty things.

Being Universal

Nationalism is incompatible with our institutions. That is why we must never hold an unfavorable attitude toward those from another country. We must never argue about politics nor wars and disputes, in case merely alluding to them should harm charity.

Nationalism goes against the words, "Go, therefore, and make disciples of all the nations" (Mt 28:19). Our heart should look like St. Paul's, which was "the heart of the whole world." Our congregation is to be open to young women from any and all nationalities.

Poverty

When one comes in touch with money, one loses contact with God. May God keep us from that; death is to be preferred.

What can be done with surplus money? Invest it in the bank? No, let us not fall into the habits of the money-lender. We have not the least reason for that, for God is watching over us.

One day there springs up the desire for money and for all that money can provide—the superfluous, luxury in eating, luxury in dressing, trifles. Needs increase because one thing calls for another. The result is uncontrollable dissatisfaction.

If you have to go shopping, pick up the simplest things. We have to be happy with our poverty. Let us not be driven by our small egotisms.

It may happen that we have to carry water up to a given floor for a bath and that we find three full buckets; the temptation then comes to use all of the water. If you have to sleep in a poorly ventilated facility, do not give signs of suffocation or difficult breathing, so as to give the impression that you are uncomfortable. It is there that poverty lies.

Poverty makes us free. Therefore we are to rejoice, smile, and have a cheerful heart.

The Creator's Thirst

"I am thirsty," said Jesus on the cross (Jn 19:28). His thirst was not for water but for love.

Our aim is to quench that thirst. With the practice of the four vows of chastity, poverty, obedience, and commitment to the poorest poor, a Missionary of Charity does not cease to quench that thirst.

St. Ignatius says, "It is no ordinary thing to satisfy the commitment you have made to tend to perfection. Consider your calling and how it is meant to be, and you will realize that those things that can satisfy others can in no way whatsoever give any satisfaction to you."

Let us be reminded also of St. Therese of Lisieux who asked, "How can I show my love, since love is manifested in actions?" She used to plant flowers: "I will not miss any sacrifice, any gesture of sensitivity, any word. . . . Doing the smallest things out of love . . . I will always sing about it, even though roses are to be taken care of in the midst of thorns. The larger and sharper the thorns, the sweeter my song will be."

Our God needs our love, but he does not need our actions. The same God who does not need to tell us if he is hungry does not feel abashed at asking the Samaritan woman for some water to drink. He was indeed thirsty, but when he said, "Give me a drink," he who was the Creator was asking for love from his creature (see Jn 4:4-30).

Messengers of Love

In order for us to become saints we will have to suffer a great deal. Suffering begets love and life in souls.

As messengers of God's love, how full of love we are to be in order to be faithful to our name! Let us remain with Mary beside the crucified Jesus, with our chalice made up of the four vows and full of the wine of our own sacrifice.

All of our gestures should be aimed at increasing our own perfection and that of our neighbor—offering our care to the sick and to the dying, picking up and educating children who are abandoned in the streets, offering shelter to the dispossessed. Devoting oneself to the conversion of the poor in the inner city is an arduous and restless task, with no results and no reward.

Our Task

Converting means leading to God. *Sanctifying* means filling with God. Converting and sanctifying are God's work. But in his infinite mercy God has chosen the Missionaries of Charity to help him in his own work.

To be able to carry Christ's light to the poorest corners of the slums is a special favor that is granted to us, not due to any special merit on our part. The Missionaries of Charity are willing to devote themselves without rest to search for the dying in the darkest, poorest, and most abandoned places.

Concern is the demonstration of God's true love. We cannot help but let ourselves be burned with the fervent desire to save souls.

Diligence, eagerness, fervor, is the test of love; and the test of fervor is the willingness to devote one's own life to working for souls. We must not feel attached to a single place; we must be willing to go all over the world.

Obedience

One cannot hide the fact that active life is full of risks because of the numerous opportunities that it offers for sin. But we can be confident of God's special protection in every action we carry out under the sign of obedience.

Doubting when obedience calls you to action is something that deserves the reproach of Jesus to Peter: "How little faith you have! Why did you falter?" (Mt 14:31).

Action and Contemplation

Our Lady set out eagerly toward the hilly region. She remained there for three months in order to carry out a servant's work on behalf of her elderly cousin.

We have to possess before we can give. He who has the mission of giving to others must grow first in the knowledge of God. He must be full of that knowledge.

St. Augustine says, "Before letting his tongue speak, the apostle should lift up his soul to God in order to pour afterward what he has drunk and to give that of which he is full."

St. Thomas Aquinas says, "Those who have been called to action would be wrong to think that they are dispensed of contemplative life. Both tasks go closely together. Thus, these two lives, far from being mutually exclusive, involve one another, carrying with them the same means and helps and being mutually complemented. If action is to be fruitful, it needs contemplative life. And the latter, when it reaches a given degree of intensity, spreads part of its surplus over the first."

When speaking is due, we should not be afraid. Someone inside will tell us what we are to say and how we should say it.

Christ must be preached in such a way that we can say to pagans that they can get to know him, to heretics and schismatics that they can come back to the right path, to lax Catholics that they can obtain his mercy, and to the good and pious that they can let themselves be consumed by his love.

Mary, under her son's guidance, has absolute sovereignty over the distribution of God's grace and favors. She is our mother because she contributes to our spiritual rebirth. And she continues to be our mother by sustaining her life in us.

Giving Oneself Tirelessly

A Missionary of Charity is a messenger of God's love, a living lamp that offers its light to all, and the salt of the earth. We are to take Christ to those places where he has not yet been taken.

The sisters ought to feed only one desire: Jesus. We must not be afraid to do what he has done. We must courageously face danger and death itself for his love and with his help.

A Missionary will always carry Christ's interest in her heart and in her spirit. The fire of love must be lodged in her heart. This love forces her to give herself tirelessly. This becomes her aim and her glory.

Missionaries

A missionary must die every day if she wants to lead souls to God.

The title *missionary religious sister* should make us feel humble since we do not deserve it.

Charity toward All

Charity is patient; it is kind; it is not jealous; it is not malicious, arrogant, or insolent. It is not self-seeking and never aims at evil. It is not pleased with the suffering of others; it rejoices in the victories of good; it has faith and hope and stands until the end (see 1 Cor 13:4-7).

The hem of love's garment touches the dust. It sweeps the stains in streets and alleys; it does so because it must.

A Missionary of Charity must be full of charity toward her own soul and must spread this charity both among Christians and among pagans.

NINE

Smiling at Jesus

Following is Mother Teresa's address during an ecumenical service at the National Presbyterian Church of Washington, D.C., in 1974.

I thank heaven for this opportunity to meet you and to ask all of you to share God's gift of acknowledging the poor. Acknowledgment leads us to love, and love will lead us to the service of the poor themselves.

The poor are the hope of salvation for mankind. As we have read, in the last judgment we will be judged according to what we have been toward them and what we have done for them. Christ's words here are transparent; we only need to interpret them in the authentic context in which he uttered them.

When Christ speaks about hunger, he is referring not merely to hunger for bread but to hunger for love, for understanding, for kindness. Christ was well aware of what it means to be unwanted because "to his own he came, yet his own did not accept him" (Jn 1:11). He also knew what it means to feel lonely, abandoned, to not have anyone to acknowledge him.

This is a hunger that affects the whole world today—a hunger that breaks many lives, that destroys many homes. There is dispossession not simply from a dwelling, from shelter, but also the dispossession of wanting to be understood, of wanting to receive mercy, of wanting someone to open his heart and welcome the one who is alone, of having nobody whom one can regard as a friend or relative.

Our sisters who live in Harlem in New York work in a jail. When teenage girls are finally able to get out of jail, there is often no one to open his heart to welcome them. A consequence is that they have to return to jail. This is a genuine dispossession.

All of us who belong to Christ—and all of us belong to him since we are all brothers and sisters, coming from the same loving hand of God—all of us have to publicly acknowledge who the poor are.

Some weeks ago, around midnight, I heard the cry of a child at our door. I went down to see the poor creature. I don't think he was more than seven years old. Sobbing inconsolably, he said to me, "I went to my father, and he didn't want me. I went to my mother, and she would not accept me either. Please love me, you at least."

That was a child's suffering—the breakdown of a family. A child who was not welcomed by his father or his mother. We have thousands of cases like that, I can assure you. There are unwanted and neglected people everywhere.

Not even God can fill what is already full. Hence we have to empty our hearts in order to allow him to fill us with his love and with his kindness.

In 1973 I accompanied my sisters to Ethiopia. The emperor asked me, "What are the sisters going to do here? What can they accomplish?"

I answered, "They will offer your people the love and kindness of Jesus."

He replied, "This is something new, a new coming of Christ."

The sisters are now there, and they do only this: they

feed Christ who is hungry, they clothe Christ who is naked, they offer shelter to Christ who is dispossessed.

In order to carry out this task, in order to continue doing his work of submission and of full commitment to God from a loving and joyful trust, our sisters lead a life of prayer and sacrifice. Our lives are consecrated to Jesus and to the Eucharist. Faith and love flowing from the Eucharist predispose us to discover Christ under the humble appearances of the poor. In this way there is but one love for us, namely Jesus, just as there is but one person in the poor, Jesus.

We profess vows. The vow of chastity enables us to love Christ with an undivided love. The vow of poverty frees us from all material worries, from the possession of every material good; in this freedom too we are able to love Christ with an undivided love.

From this vow of undivided love, we commit ourselves completely through the person who occupies Christ's position—hence our vow of obedience, which is another way of giving, of loving.

Then comes our fourth vow, which consists in the solemn commitment we make to offer wholeheartedly a free service to the poorest poor—that is, to Christ under the humble appearances of the poor. We commit ourselves to be one with the poorest poor, to depend exclusively on divine providence, to possess nothing even though we possess everything as we possess Christ.

Because of this vow, we have in India and elsewhere—for example, in Bangladesh, Australia, Africa, Latin America, and Harlem—houses for the unwanted, for the abandoned, for the sick and the dying, for small children, for paralytics, for the blind. We have also picked up thousands of lepers, who are the most unwanted, the sick whom all people avoid.

We have alcoholics and afflicted people of all kinds. We

welcome people who know only two places—the jail and the street. We have orphanages and caring centers for newborn babies.

None of these things represent for us a waste of time, even though we take care of small and seemingly irrelevant things like feeding the hungry, washing their clothes, or affectionately caring for the unwanted.

Some months ago an alcoholic man was picked up by the sisters on the streets of Melbourne. He had been in that condition for several years.

The sisters took him to the House of Mercy. Their care of him made him realize that God loved him. He left the house and never again tasted alcohol. He returned to his family and his job.

Later, when the man received his first paycheck, he came back to the sisters and said to them, "I want you to be God's love for others too. I want you to do for them as you have done for me."

Such a simple job! What counts is not what we do, nor the amount of things we do, but the love we put into our actions, since those actions are our love for God in action.

Some weeks back one of our brothers came to me in anguish and said, "My calling is to work for the lepers." He really loved the lepers. "I want to devote my life, my whole being, to carry out that calling," he said.

I replied, "You are mistaken, Brother. Your calling is to belong to Jesus. He has chosen you for himself, and work is only a means of love for him in action. So the work you carry out is of no importance. What is important is that you belong to him, that you are his, that he gives you the means to do what you have to do."

The same is true for us: it does not matter what we do or where we are, as long as we bear in mind that we are his belonging, that Jesus can do with us whatever he wants, that we owe him our love, and that we love him. Whether we work for the rich or on behalf of the poor, whether we work among people of high society or among inhabitants of the inner city, what is important is only the love we put into carrying out our job.

Maybe you and I are the only ones through whom Jesus can come to those whom we are touching. Because in the rich, it is not that we love the preciousness of their gifts but that our love addresses the person who belongs to God, the child of God who is our brother and our sister.

Therefore, let us try to spread this love of Christ—above all in our own family, among our own, my husband, my wife, my children. Does my home, my community, burn in love? Do I have time to devote to my sisters? Do I have time for my children, for my husband, for my wife?

I cannot forget my mother. She was usually very busy all day long. But when sunset drew near, it was her custom to hurry with her tasks in order to be ready to receive my father. At the time we did not understand, and we would smile and even joke a little about it. Today I cannot help but call to mind that great delicacy of love that she had for him. No matter what happened, she was always prepared, with a smile on her lips, to welcome him.

Today we have no time. Fathers and mothers are so busy that when children come home they are not welcomed with love or with a smile.

Some visitors to Calcutta asked me to tell them something that would be useful for them to lead their lives in a more profitable way.

I answered, "Smile at each other. Smile at your wives, at your husbands, at your children, at all, without looking at the one at whom you are smiling. Let mutual love for others grow each day in all of you."

At this point one of them asked me, "Are you married?"

I answered, "Yes, I am married to Jesus. And sometimes it is difficult for me to smile at him because he is too demanding."

It is true: sometimes Jesus can ask too much of you. But it is in such moments that our smile becomes more beautiful.

This is really what Jesus asks us to do: to love each other as the Father has loved him. And how did the Father love Christ? Through sacrifice: he delivered him to death for our salvation.

If we really want to conquer the world, we will not be able to do it with bombs or with other weapons of destruction. Let us conquer the world with our love. Let us interweave our lives with bonds of sacrifice and love, and it will be possible for us to conquer the world.

The poor are great and lovable people. It is often they who deserve our greatest gratitude, since they are so wonderful in their ability to endure and to suffer. Were it not for the suffering of so many innocent people, I do not know what would become of the world. We receive a great deal from those we help, from contact with them, because it is nothing less than contact with the body of Christ twenty-four hours a day.

Pray for us. Pray for those we aid. And pray for our sisters, our brothers, and our co-workers, that we will not waste God's work because of our selfishness, thinking it is we and not he working through us, who carries out everything by means of us, in us, and with us.

TEN

Unity Will Make Us Stronger

These are Mother Teresa's words given at the National Shrine of the Immaculate Conception in Washington, D.C., on October 26, 1975.

I want to thank each and every one of you for what you have done throughout these years, through Catholic Relief Services, in order to share the joy of serving the poorest poor.

God so loved the world that he gave his Son that he would be one of us, like unto us in everything except in sin. His Son, Jesus Christ, loved you and loved me. And he became the bread of life in order to meet the hunger for God that fills our hearts.

But this was not enough for him: he wanted to put this love of God in living action. He became hungry, naked, sick, dispossessed, needing help. He became unwanted, unloved, so that you and I might be able to have the joy of feeding him, of clothing him, of offering him shelter, or entrusting him with our love, of making him feel loved, of making him feel that he is someone very special for you and for me.

This Jesus—this Jesus who is hungry for love and for

bread, this Jesus who is deprived of food and of human dignity, this Jesus who lacks a home and understanding love—this Jesus is present today everywhere in the world, even here in the United States. He is looking at you and me and asking, "Do you love me? Are you willing to wipe out this suffering, which is the suffering of thousands and thousands of human beings all over the world—beings who lack not only bread but love, who want to be understood and acknowledged as our brothers and sisters, who are created by the same loving hand of God?"

In India, in Africa, but even in the United States, there can be people who are sunken in loneliness. There can be people like that in our own house, in our own family. Are we aware of that?

Especially today, when the world is so busy and people are always in a hurry, it seems we have no time to smile at each other, to devote a little time to others, to our neighbor. And thus loneliness grows every day. How much loneliness there is in the homes of shut-ins, those who can't go out.

In order to do what they do, our sisters need to know what poverty is. They need to know it as a way of life in order to know and love the poor.

That is why the sisters have their religious vows. They commit themselves fully to Jesus, in order to love him with an undivided love in chastity, through the freedom of their poverty, in full submission through obedience, and in an absolutely voluntary and gratuitous service to the poorest poor—that is to say, to Christ in his most humble appearance.

Our lives have to continuously feed on the Eucharist. If we were not able to see Christ under the appearance of bread, neither would it be possible for us to discover him under the humble appearances of the bruised bodies of the poor.

God's work needs both you and me. Let us carry out this work together. Let us all together do something beautiful for God. What you can do we cannot do, and what we are doing you cannot accomplish. Together we will be able to accomplish and fulfill something beautiful for God through our full commitment and through our loving trust and joy in service to God through service to the poorest poor.

Our sisters, as well as our poor, depend entirely on divine providence, who through us cares for thousands and thousands of people who are spread all over the world. To this day we have never had to reject anyone because of lacking a bed, some medicine, or some other need.

We have to love Christ to the point of hurting. I do not want you to give your surplus. I want you to sacrifice something you love, like that child I have mentioned in other circumstances who deprived himself of sugar in order to give it to our orphans. It was a great gesture for such a small child to love to the point of depriving himself of something.

Do we know our poor here? Do we really know them? Unless we know them, we cannot love them. And if we do not love them, we cannot serve them. Knowledge leads to love, and love to service.

Remember us in your prayers, so that we will be able to be united with Christ through prayer and sacrifice. This is the ideal of the young sisters who embrace the life of our congregation, something which is really very beautiful. We want to undertake a life of poverty, of prayer, and of sacrifice that will lead us to the service of the poor.

Pray also for your children, that Christ's calling and choice may rest upon your families for a vocation to the priesthood or to religious life. It is a gift from God to a family.

ELEVEN

Joyful Self-Giving

Our Father

You should make all effort to walk in the presence of God, to see God in all persons you meet, to live out your morning meditation throughout the day.

When you go out for your task, spread all around you the joy of belonging to God, of living with God, of being his own. In the streets, in the poor neighborhoods, at work, pray always with all your heart and all your soul. Keep the silence which Jesus kept throughout thirty years of life in Nazareth and which he continues to keep today in the tabernacle, interceding for us. Pray as Mary did, for she kept all things in her heart, through prayer and meditation, and she continues to be a mediatrix of all graces.

Christ's teaching is so simple that even a very young child can babble it. The Apostles asked, "Teach us to pray." Jesus answered, "When you pray say, '*Our Father* . . .'" (See Luke 11:1-4).

Trusting God

We can sincerely muster our courage and say, "In him who is the source of my strength I have strength for everything" (Phil 4:13).

According to this statement of St. Paul, you should trust in the success of your work, which is rather God's work, with the effectiveness and perfection of Jesus and through Jesus. Be assured that by yourselves you can do nothing and have nothing, except sin, weakness, and misery. All our natural gifts and those that come from grace have been gratuitously offered us by God.

One can see Jesus' humility in the manger, in the flight to Egypt, in his hidden life, in the impossibility of making himself understood by men. We see it in the abandonment of the Apostles, in his rejection by the Jews, in the overwhelming pain of his passion. Currently we see it in his acts of constant humility in the tabernacle, where he is reduced to a piece of bread so tiny that the priest can hold it in his hands.

God's Instruments

Christ's life was not written while he was living, even though he accomplished the most important work that exists: redeeming the world and teaching mankind to love his Father. Our work is Christ's work, and so we have to be his instruments, to carry out our small task and to disappear.

Messengers of Love

Let there be no pride or vanity in our work. It is God's work, and the poor are his poor. Let us place ourselves completely under the influence of Jesus, so that he may think through our spirit and work through our hands. We can do everything if his strength is in us.

Our mission is to convey God's love—not a dead God but a living one.

Love: the First Thing

People think we are only asking for money. It is not money that I am interested in.

We strive to live out concretely the love of Christ in each of our actions every day, despite our weaknesses and miseries. Every day we are in touch with the most marginal of society. More than money, what these people need is our heart.

"Love Each Other. . ."

All human beings are brothers and sisters. All of us have been created by the same loving hand of God. Jesus has said to us all, "Love one another as I have loved you" (Jn 15:12). And he has also said, "As the Father has loved me, so love one another" (see Jn 15:9).

Having this command of Jesus, we cannot be known for a party spirit.

Each One's Mission

In the world there are some who struggle for justice and human rights. We have no time for this because we are in daily and continuous contact with men who are starving for a piece of bread to put in their mouth and for some affection. Should I devote myself to struggle for the justice of tomorrow or even for the justice of today, the most needy people would die right in front of me because they lack a glass of milk.

Nevertheless, I want to state clearly that I do not condemn those who struggle for justice. I believe there are different options for the people of God. To me the most important is to serve the neediest people.

Within the church some do one thing, others do a

different thing. What is important is that all of us remain united, each one of us developing his own specific task.

The Vine and the Branches

Let us be like a genuine and fruitful branch of the vine, which is Christ, accepting him in our lives the way he gives himself to us: as truth, which must be spoken; as life, which must be lived; as light, which must shine out; as love, which must be loved; as a way, which must be trodden; as joy, which must be communicated; as peace, which must be radiated; as sacrifice, which must be offered in our families, to our closest neighbors, and to those who live far away.

Love

Love is a fruit in season at all times.

Prayer

We must love prayer. It widens the heart to the point of making it capable of containing the gift that God makes of himself. Ask and seek, and your heart will be widened to welcome him and to keep him within itself.

Love of Neighbor

At the time of death, when we meet God face-to-face, we will be judged concerning love, concerning how much we have loved. Not concerning how much we have accomplished, but rather how much love we have put into what we have done.

In order for love to be genuine, it has to be above all a love for my neighbor. Love for my neighbor will lead me to true love for God. What the sisters, the brothers, and the co-workers try to do all over the world is to put into loving action their love for God.

Mutual Need

The poor need us, but the need we have for the poor is no less.

The Sickness of Lovelessness

There are many medicines and cares for all kinds of sick people. But unless kind hands are given in service and generous hearts are given in love, I do not think there can ever be any cure for the terrible sickness of feeling unloved.

Small Instruments

Each one of us is merely a small instrument; all of us, after accomplishing our mission, will disappear.

Way, Truth, Love

Let us make every effort to grow spiritually into the image of Christ, in order to allow him to lead his life of mercy and humanness in today's world.

Your love for Christ is very great. Keep the light of Christ always shining in your hearts. Only he is the way to be trodden. He is the truth we must speak out. He is the love we must love.

To Sick Co-workers

How happy I feel because of you! Often, when my work is very hard, I think about you and say to Jesus, "Look at these children of yours who suffer, and bless my work for their sake." I feel instantly comforted.

You see, you are our hidden treasure, the secret strength of the Missionaries of Charity. I personally feel very happy, and a new strength comes over my soul, as I think of all those who are spiritually united to us. With your collaboration and help, what won't we be able to accomplish for him! Your lives are like a shining lamp which burns for souls.

The Intensity of Love

There are poor people everywhere, but the deepest poverty is not being loved. The poor whom we must seek may live near us or far away. They can be materially or spiritually poor. They may be hungry for bread or hungry for friendship. They may need clothing, or they may need the sense of wealth that God's love for them represents. They may need the shelter of a house made of bricks and cement or the shelter of having a place in our hearts.

We do not need to carry out grand things in order to show a great love for God and for our neighbor. It is the intensity of love we put into our gestures that makes them into something beautiful for God.

The Need for God

Money is not enough. I do not want anyone to offer me money which I can get if I ask for it. My poor need to be loved with the heart and to be served with the hands.

Christ uses me as an instrument to put you in touch with his poor. This is what I think happens when I go wherever I am called: many people are joined together by the sense of the common need for God.

A Lesson in Humility

May God give back to you in love all the love you have given and all the joy and peace you have sown around you, all over the world. May God bless you deeply.

All of us must intend to work in a special way for the sake of peace. In order to bring about that peace, all of us must learn from Jesus to be meek and humble of heart. Only humility will lead us to unity, and unity to peace.

Let us help each other get as close to Jesus as possible. This is the lesson of humility which we must learn.

The Poor near Us

We must love those who are nearest to us, in our own family. From there, love spreads toward whomever may need us.

We must try to discover the poor in our own setting because only if we know them will we be able to understand them and to offer them our love. And only when we love them will we be willing to offer them our service of love.

To the Incurably Sick

You, the incurably sick, can do much for the poor. You are crucified with Christ every day. You sprinkle our work with your prayer, and you help us offer others the strength to work.

Jesus and the Poor

God so loved the world that he gave his Son to die for the world. Jesus said, "As the Father has loved me, so I

have loved you . . . Love one another as I have loved you"
(Jn 15:9, 12).

The gift was from the Father and from the Son. Now
the gift must be from us.

Jesus identified himself with those who are hungry,
with those who are sick, with those who are naked, with
those who have no shelter: hungry not only for bread but
for love, for care, for being meaningful to somebody;
deprived not only of clothing but of that compassion that
only a few are able to offer to those who do not know each
other; dispossessed not only of a house of brick and clay
but of the possibility of being considered a relative or
friend of someone.

The Young Women of Bangladesh

We must pray for those countries that have passed laws
that accept abortion as a natural action. This is a
transgression! Their sin is great.

When we were invited to take care of the young women
of Bangladesh who had been raped by soldiers, we saw the
need to open a home for children. The difficulties were
great because accepting in society young women who had
been raped went against both Hindu and Moslem laws.
But when the leader of Bangladesh said that those young
women were heroines of the nation—who had fought for
their own purity, who had struggled for their country—
their very parents came to look for them. In many cases we
were able to find young men who offered to marry them.

Some people favored abortion. It was a terrible
struggle, if I can say it that way, that we had to fight with
them. I told them that the young women had been
violated, that they did not want to sin; whereas now what
the men wanted to do was to force them or to help them
to commit a transgression that would accompany them
throughout their lives. I told them that these mothers
would never forget that they had killed their own
children.

Thanks be to God, the government accepted our conditions. The people were told that each of the children for whom abortion would have been chosen should be taken to the house of Mother Teresa to receive help. Of the forty children we received, more than thirty went to Canada and other countries, adopted by generous families.

The Greatness of the Poor

The indifference of people who walk by without picking up those whom we pick up is a confirmation of their ignorance and lack of faith. If they were convinced that the one who is lying on the ground is their brother or their sister, I think they would undoubtedly do something. Unfortunately, they do not know what compassion is and they do not know those beings.

If they understood them, they would immediately become aware of the greatness of those human beings who are lying on the sidewalks. They would love them naturally, and loving them would lead them to serve them. I can assert that those who really commit themselves to knowing the poor soon realize that the poor are our brothers, no matter what their race, nationality, or religion is.

We the Missionaries of Charity carry out an offensive of love, of prayer, of sacrifice on behalf of the poorest poor. We want to conquer the world through love, and thus bring to everyone's heart the love of God and the proof that God loves the world.

Love of Predilection

The aim of the Missionaries of Charity is to take God, to take his love, to the homes of the poor and thus to lead them to him. It does not matter who they are, nor what their nationality or social status may be. We intend to make them understand the love and compassion that God has for them, which is a love of predilection.

Loving Those Who Are Near

It is easy to love those who live far away. It is not always easy to love those who live right next to us. It is easier to offer a dish of rice to meet the hunger of a needy person than to comfort the loneliness and the anguish of someone in our own home who does not feel loved.

Contact with Jesus

After the sisters have finished their day—carrying out their service of love in the company of Jesus, for the love of Jesus, and through Jesus—we have an hour of prayer and of eucharistic adoration. Throughout the day we have been in contact with Jesus through his image of sorrow in the poor and lepers. When the day ends, we come in contact with him again in the tabernacle by means of prayer.

God in the Poor

The poor are the hope of mankind. Those who suffer hunger and trouble, those who do not feel loved—we will be judged according to how we have treated them, according to the love we have offered them.

They are our hope of salvation. We have to come close to each one of them and treat each one of them as we would treat Jesus himself. It does not matter who they are or where they are: we must see God in them.

Listening

The first listening groups have begun to bud among our co-workers. Those who make up these groups visit the elderly—sometimes in very common and poor houses—and sit down, just letting them talk on and on. The elderly enjoy having someone who listens to them, even when the things they have to say go back to twenty or thirty years ago. Listening, when no one else volunteers to do it, is no doubt a very noble thing.

Gestures of Love

No one should avoid the smallest tasks. Any task of love is a task of peace, no matter how insignificant it may seem.

In the world there is too much hatred, too much fighting. We will not be able to put them away with guns or bombs or any kind of weapon that wounds. We will attain that only through gestures of love, joy, and peace.

The Thrust of Love

If there is today some crisis of credibility concerning Catholic or Catholic-inspired organizations, the causes may be found in a lack of zeal and of the motives that must be a basis for building a work of charity. As long as love and godliness shape the work of charity, no work will ever fail because of financial reasons. On the other hand, as soon as this thrust of love and godliness is lost, every work is doomed.

Abundance of Vocations

A vocation is a gift of Christ. He has said, "I have chosen you." Every vocation must really belong to Christ. The work that we are called to accomplish is just a means to give concrete substance to our love for God.

Young women today are seeking something to which they can commit everything. They are convinced that a life of poverty, of prayer, of sacrifice—which will be of help to them in the service of their neighbor, of the poorest poor—is the answer to their desires, their aspirations, their hopes.

I think they see in our congregation this life of poverty, of prayer, and of sacrifice. In our work on behalf of the poorest poor they see carried into action the Lord's words, "I was hungry and you fed me; I was naked and you clothed me; I was homeless and you welcomed me" (see Mt 25: 35,36). This is what we, in the anguish and sorrow of the poor, try to do for Christ.

To Christ through the Poor

Our life is linked to the Eucharist. Through faith in and love of the body of Christ under the appearance of bread, we take Christ literally: "I was hungry and you gave me food. I was a stranger and you welcomed me, naked and you clothed me."

The particular aim of our congregation is to offer wholehearted free service to the poorest poor, to Christ in the semblance of those who suffer. The work we carry out is only our love for Christ in concrete action.

That is why we strive to love Christ with an undivided love in chastity, through the freedom of poverty, in total submission in obedience, and in cordial service to the poorest poor—to Christ under the semblance of those who suffer. These are the four vows we proclaim, and they make the essential difference in our life.

We are not mere social assistants, but we try to be contemplatives in the midst of the world because we take Christ literally. Jesus has said, "I was hungry and you gave me food." Therefore we remain in his presence twenty-four hours a day, by being in touch with the poor.

God Helps Us

Concerning the economic means for supporting our works of charity, we live by the words of Jesus. He said, "the Father cares for you and knows your needs. In his eyes, you are more important than the lilies of the field or the birds of the sky" (see Mt 6:26-34).

We have never had to reject anyone for lack of resources. The good God has always shown the most delicate care and a love full of tenderness for the poor, using us to offer them out of the abundance of his love.

The Eucharist and the Poor

Faith in action is love, and love in action is service. Jesus has said, "I was hungry, I was naked, homeless.... You did it for me." We take Christ at his word, and we believe in him.

We need the Eucharist because Jesus has become the bread of life in order to meet our desires, our longings, our love for him. This is why our life needs to be closely linked to the Eucharist. We begin our day with the holy mass and communion, and we finish the day with an hour of adoration, which unites us with Jesus and with the poor in whom we offer our services.

The Reward of the Poor

As long as there are some who are rich, there will also be others who are poor. Jesus has said it: "The poor you always have with you" (Jn 12:8).

We need to understand the poor. There is not only material poverty but also spiritual poverty, which is harder and deeper, harboring even in the hearts of very wealthy men. Wealth is not only property and money, but our attachment to these things and our abuse of them.

When things become our masters, we are very poor. And so as long as there are rich people who commit excess and do not use things according to the mind of God, there will be poverty in the world.

Our work has awakened a new awareness in the hearts

of many, so that today no one can ignore the existence of the poor, of the hungry, of those who suffer from cold. As people learn about our work, they become aware that the poor are our brothers and sisters and that we have to show concern and consideration for their situation.

For my part, I must say that the poor are very lovable people, who give us more, much more, than we give them. We must know them. Knowledge will lead us to love; love will lead us to service. They do not need our compassion or condescendence—they need our love. Therefore we are to serve them with our hands and love them with our hearts.

Providence

We depend solely on divine providence. Christ has said that we are more important in his eyes than the flowers, the grass, and the birds. He is concerned for those we help.

We care for thousands of people in India and elsewhere, and up to now we have always had something to give. We have never been forced to dismiss anyone because of lack of space or food. God has always been present with his love and concern.

The Freedom of the Poor

Death, in the final analysis, is only the easiest and quickest means to go back to God. If only we could make people understand that we come from God and that we have to go back to him!

Everyone knows that we have not been created by ourselves. Someone else has created us. Going back to him is going back home.

We sisters face death almost every day. It is beautiful to

see people who die with dignity, radiating joy at going back to the place they came from, at going back to the only One who loves them.

Those who have had many possessions, who have had many goods and riches, are obsessed by them. They think that the only thing that counts is possessing wealth. That is why it is so difficult for them to leave all things. It is much easier for the poor, who are so free, for this freedom allows them to depart with joy.

The Dignity of the Poor

The poor are wonderful people. They have their own dignity, which we can easily see.

Usually the poor are not known, and therefore one is not able to discover their dignity. But the poor have above all great courage to lead the life they lead. They are forced to live like that; poverty has been imposed on them. We choose poverty; they are forced to accept it.

Giving Ourselves to God

Total abandonment consists of giving oneself fully to God because God has given himself to us. If God, who owes us nothing, is willing to give us nothing less than himself, can we respond by giving him only a part of ourselves? Renouncing myself, I give myself to God that he might live in me.

How poor we would be if God had not given us the power to give ourselves over to him! Instead, how rich we are right now!

How easy it is to conquer God! We give ourselves to him, and God becomes ours, and now we have nothing but God. The prize with which God rewards our self-abandonment is himself.

Closer to Christ

Renouncing means to offer my free will, my reason, my life, in an attitude of faith. My soul can be in darkness; trials are the surest tests of my blind renunciation.

Renunciation also means love. The more we renounce, the more we love God and man.

If we really love men, we must be willing to take their places, to take responsibility for their sins and to expiate them. We must be living holocausts, since men need that.

God's love has no limits. Its depth is unfathomable: "I will not leave you orphaned" (Jn 14:18).

Let's turn the image around. There should also be no limits to the love that impels us to give ourselves over to God and to become victims of his love. The common and ordinary cannot be enough for us. That which is good for others is not enough for us. We have to quench God's thirst by dying for love. Not content with the common good, but with a courage that will face all dangers with a serene soul, willing at all times to make any sacrifice, to accomplish any task or work, the Missionary of Charity must at all times be committed to be as close as possible to her king who is dying of thirst.

Trust

Jesus wants us to put all our trust in him. We have to renounce our desires in order to work for our own perfection. Even if we feel like a boat without a compass on the high seas, we are to commit ourselves fully to him, without trying to control his actions.

I cannot long for a clear perception of my progress along the route, nor long to know precisely where I am on the path of holiness. I ask Jesus to make me a saint. I leave it to him to choose the means that can lead me in that direction.

Our Joy

Joy must be one of the pivots of our life. It is the token of a generous personality. Sometimes it is also a mantle that clothes a life of sacrifice and self-giving.

A person who has this gift often reaches high summits. He or she is like a sun in a community. Let those who suffer find in us comforting angels.

Why has the work in the slums been blessed by God? Certainly not because of given personal qualities, but because of the joy that the sisters spread as they pass by.

The people of the world lack our joy. Those who live in the slums have still less of it. Our joy is the best means to preach Christianity to the heathen.

The Silence of Jesus

Let us admire Christ's compassion toward Judas. The Master kept a holy silence: he did not want to reveal his betrayer in front of his comrades.

Jesus could have easily spoken out and unveiled the hidden intentions of Judas. He preferred mercy rather than condemnation. He called him *friend*. If Judas had looked in Jesus' eyes, he would surely have been the friend of God's mercy.

A Crisis Purifies

The church is undergoing difficult times. Do not let yourselves be disturbed by gossip. You will hear about priests and nuns who abandon their vocations, about homes that are broken. Do not forget that there are thousands and thousands of faithful priests, nuns, and families.

This trial will purify the church of human illnesses, in order for it to arise more beautiful and authentic.

Christ's Humiliation

Christ continues to look for someone to offer him consolation. Are we trying to do that?

Nowadays Christ is being humiliated in the person of his Vicar, through prideful actions of disobedience and disloyalty. He is being oppressed by wrong speech.

Christ is thirsty for gentleness; he is begging that of you. He is despoiled of the loyalty that he expects from you.

The suffering of the church is caused by a misunderstanding of freedom and renewal. We cannot be free unless we are able to renounce our own will for Christ's. We cannot be renewed without the humility to recognize what needs to be renewed in ourselves. Distrust those who come to you with dazzling words about freedom and renewal: they are deceivers.

The Passion of Calcutta

Calcutta really partakes in Christ's passion. It is sad to see so many miseries in our beloved city. But Calcutta will become better and will be the mother of the poor.

Our mission there, *Shanti Nagar,* will be transformed into what its name says: a magnificent "Village of Peace."

Poverty as Guarantee

There are sisters who seem to constantly worry that we may run out of resources for the work. When you request something, never give the impression that you are raising money. Let your work speak for you. Let your love strike the hearts of those who are better off; they will be generous.

Even if you have to beg, show your detachment by feeling comfortable, both when nothing is given you and when you receive generously. A rich man in Delhi used to say, "How beautiful it is to see these sisters so free from the world in the twentieth century, when it seems that all things except the modern ones are out of fashion."

Remain on the simple paths of poverty, repairing your own shoes, loving poverty as a mother. We must consider ourselves especially fortunate because we have the opportunity to practice this marvelous poverty.

Our congregation will live as long as this real poverty continues. Institutions where poverty is faithfully practiced have no reason to fear decadence.

When St. Francis of Assisi learned that a rich house had been built for the brothers, he refused to enter it. We must not occupy our time in trying to make our houses beautiful and attractive. May God keep us free of convents with rich furniture, where the poor would feel strange to enter for fear that their poverty would be a dishonor.

When we clean ourselves, we must be aware of the significance of each of the elements of our apparel: the *sari* with the blue stripe is a sign of the modesty of the Virgin; the string belt denotes purity; the sandals signify our free choice; the crucifix is a symbol of love.

The Extreme Poverty of Jesus

The sisters are to live by begging. We depend fully on the charity of others. We must not be ashamed to beg from door to door, if need be. The Lord has promised a reward even for a glass of water given in his name. We become beggars for his sake.

The Lord sometimes suffered real indigence, as can be understood from the multiplication of bread and fish and the picking of grain at the edge of the path. This thought should serve as a comfort to us when our food is scarce.

On the cross Christ was deprived of everything. The cross itself had been given him by Pilate; the nails and the crown, by the soldiers. He was naked.

When he died he was stripped of the cross, the nails, and the crown. He was wrapped in a piece of canvas donated by a charitable soul, and he was buried in a tomb that did not belong to him.

Despite all that, Jesus could have died like a king and could even have been spared death. He chose poverty because he knew that it was the genuine means to possess God and to bring his love to the earth.

Serving

"Love one another." Suppress this command, and the whole work of the church of Christ will fall.

Charity toward the poor must be a burning flame in our society. Just as the fire, when it ceases burning, spreads no more warmth, so the Missionaries of Charity, should they lack love, would lose all usefulness and would have no more life.

Charity is like a living flame: the drier the fuel, the livelier the flame. Likewise our hearts, when they are free of all earthly causes, commit themselves in free service.

Love of God must give rise to a total service. The more disgusting the work is, the greater must love be, as it takes succor to the Lord disguised in the rags of the poor.

Poverty and Richness

I think that a person who is attached to riches, who lives with the worry of riches, is actually very poor. If this person puts his money at the service of others, then he is rich, very rich.

Christ's Rags

When we remember that every morning at communion we have held in our hands all the holiness of God, we feel more willing to abstain from everything that may stain our purity. Thence flows a sincere and deep respect for our own person—respect also toward others leading us to treat them with sensitivity but likewise abstaining from all disordered sentimentality.

When we are dealing with the sick, we are touching the body of Christ who suffers. This contact gives us a heroism that makes us forget all disgust.

We need a deep faith in order to see Christ in the bruised body and the dirty rags. Under them is hidden the one who is fairer in beauty than the sons of men. We need the hands of Christ in order to touch those bodies wounded by suffering.

Inner Life

True inner life makes active life burn in fervor and consumes everything. It makes us find Jesus in the darkest corners of the slums, in the saddest miseries of the poor. It puts us in touch with the Man-God who is naked on the cross—sad, despised by all, the Man of Sorrows oppressed by scourging and crucifixion.

What does the congregation expect from me? That I be a coworker of Christ.

Where can we carry out that task? Not in the houses of the rich but in the slums: there is our realm.

We cannot take charge of works that would divert us from the slums, from the neighborhoods of misery. That is the kingdom of Christ and ours—our working field. If a son abandons the field of his father and goes to work in another field, he ceases to be a coworker of his father.

Those who share everything are partners who give love for love, suffering for suffering. Jesus has given us everything—his life, his blood, everything. Now it is our turn. We cannot desert his field.

Sowers of Peace

In our work we can be attracted to idle chatter. Let us be attentive not to run this danger when we visit families. We can fall into talking about this and that, forgetting the central point of our visit.

We want to and we must take the peace of Christ: let us not be vehicles of dissension. We must never consent to anybody talking to us against his neighbors.

If we run across a family who are in a bad mood and who are prone to slide into topics that are contrary to charity, let us slip in some words to make them think a little about God. Then let us go away, for no good is possible if the nerves are excited.

We must do the same with those who make us lose precious time. If the search for God does not attract them, let us leave them. We have no time to lose.

Pluralism

There must be a great deal of pluralism in the church. Some fight for justice and human rights. We have no time for that: there are too many poor who die because they do not have a piece of bread to bring to their mouths and because they lack a bit of affection!

Giving Christ

Listen to what Jesus says: "I want you to be my fire of love among the poor, the dying, and the small. I want you to bring the poor to me." Learn this expression by heart, and repeat it when you lack generosity. We risk rejecting Jesus every time we reject others.

If our attitude is "I will not give you my hands to work, my eyes to see, my legs to walk, my spirit to study, my heart to love. You will knock at my door, but I will not open," then it is a wounded Christ, a battered Christ, a Christ of deformity that we give to others.

If you want others to love him, you must first make him known to them. So give a whole Christ to those who live in the inner city—a Christ full of love, of joy, of light. Do not be a dim light, but a shining light.

Humility

Humility is nothing but truth. "What do we have that we have not received?" asks St. Paul (see 1 Cor 4:7). And if I have received everything, what is it that I have that is mine?

If we are convinced of this, we will never lift up our heads with arrogance. If we are humble, nothing will touch us—neither praise nor contempt—for we know what we are.

Self-Knowledge

Knowing ourselves puts us in our rightful places. This knowing is necessary for love because the knowledge of God yields love, and self-knowledge yields humility.

Says St. Augustine, "Above all, fill yourselves up, and then you will be able to give to others."

Self-knowledge is very useful. The saints can sincerely say that they are great criminals. They have been able to see God and to see themselves, and they have noted the difference. That is why they are not surprised even when they are unjustly accused.

Seeking God

Belonging to a particular Christian tradition is only relevant for the individual. If the individual thinks and believes that for him this is the only way to God, if he knows no other, if he has no doubt and feels no need to continue seeking, then this is his way of salvation—this way God comes to him.

But from the moment a soul has the grace to know God, he must seek. If he does not seek, he is going astray from the just way. God offers all souls created by him an opportunity to meet him face-to-face, to accept him or to reject him.

Christian Consistency

The unity of Christians is an important thing because Christians are a light for others. If we are Christians, we must look like Christ—this is my deep conviction.

Gandhi once said that if Christians were really Christians, there would be no Hindus in India. People expect us to fully live our Christian life.

We Must Not Judge

God has his own means to work in the hearts of men, and we cannot know how close to him each man is. But through a man's actions we may know whether he is available to God or not.

It is not ours to condemn, to judge, or to pronounce hurting words. It may be that someone has never heard about Christianity; we do not know how God shows himself to that soul and how he uses it. How then could we be entitled to issue the least judgment of condemnation?

Looking at Christ

Sometimes we do not get from prayer what we are seeking because we do not focus our attention and our heart on Christ, through whom our prayers reach God.

Often a deep and fervent look at Christ is the best prayer: I look at him and he looks at me.

Generosity and Love

If our poor die of hunger, it is not because God does not care for them. Rather, it is because neither you nor I are generous enough. It is because we are not instruments of love in the hands of God to give them food and clothing. We do not recognize Christ when once again he appears to us under the appearance of suffering—in the hungry man, in the lonely, in the child who is looking for a place where he can get warm.

Faith and Generosity

Faith is a gift from God. Without faith, no life is possible. For our work to bear fruit, for it to belong to God alone, it must be founded on faith.

Christ has said, "I was hungry, naked, sick, homeless. . . . You did it for me" (see Mt 25:35-40). Our work is founded on faith in these words of Christ.

Faith is scarce nowadays because selfishness is quite abundant; personal advantage is sought above all. Faith cannot be genuine without being generous. Love and faith go together; they complement each other.

The Challenge of Youth

It is the young people who will build the world of tomorrow. Today's youth are looking for the challenge of self-denial.

A young man from a rich family in New York came in his car to our residence and told me, "I have given everything to the poor, and I have come to follow Christ."

Unexpected Details

Jesus has unexpected details sometimes.

Once, in London, I received a telephone call from the police: "Mother Teresa, there is a woman in the street, reeking of alcohol, who is asking for you." We went to pick her up.

As we were coming back she said, "Mother Teresa, Christ changes water into wine in order to give us to drink." She was, indeed, very drunk.

God's Judgment

All of us have just as much good as bad in ourselves. Let no one boast of his own successes but ascribe them to God.

We must never consider ourselves indispensable. God has his own designs, but he wants our love. We can lose our life to carry out our mission, but if it is not pervaded by love it will be useless.

God does not need our work. He will not ask us how many books we have read or how many miracles we have worked but only whether we have done what we could out of love.

The Value of Things

If you feel discouraged, sisters, it is a sign of pride. It is an obvious proof of your excessive self-confidence.

Do not worry about others' opinions of you. Be humble and do not let yourselves ever be disturbed.

St. Aloysius Gonzaga used to say that he would continue to play billiards, even if he knew that death was imminent. Have you played, eaten, and slept? These are duties: nothing is small in God's sight.

Poor Like Jesus

It would be a shame for us to be richer than Jesus, who for our sake endured poverty.

Love and Prayer

Our prayers should be delicious and hot victuals that come from the fire of a heart overflowing with love.

Poverty and Charity

Our lives have to be more and more penetrated by a deep faith in Jesus, the bread of life, which must be eaten with and for the poor.

Are we really the poorest among the poor? With poverty, which frees us, charity will also grow.

Jesus in the Heart

I desire for you the joy of the Virgin, who because she was humble in her heart, was able to keep Jesus in her womb for nine months. What a long communion!

The Spirit of Sacrifice

Jesus has chosen each one of us to be his love and his light in the world. The spirit of sacrifice will always be the salt of our society.

Reconciliation

Reconciliation begins with ourselves. It begins with a pure heart, a heart that is able to see God in others.

The tongue, that part of the body that makes such

direct contact with the body of Christ, can become an instrument of joy or of suffering. Do not go to bed when you know that your sister has something against you.

Forgiving

The government of Bangladesh has asked us to take care of young women who have been raped. I want to call your attention to what Mujib Rahman, the leader of that country, has said about these young women: "They will be treated like national heroines because they have suffered unspeakably to defend their purity."

These young women, Hindus and Moslems, because of their natural love of purity, have had to struggle to protect themselves. Many of them even committed suicide because of the fear of losing this beautiful virtue of womanhood.

We, as religious sisters who have consecrated to God this wonderful gift of virginity, must take care of these women in order to protect them. If we do not forgive, it will be a sign that we have not been forgiven.

The Silence of Jesus

Today, when everything is up for discussion, let us go back to Nazareth. How surprising it is that Jesus spent thirty years without doing anything—without "giving himself an opportunity."

At twelve years of age this boy Jesus silenced the priests in the temple with his answers. But in thirty years we know nothing else about him, except that everyone was surprised when they saw him appear in public: "Isn't this the carpenter's son?" (Mt 13:55).

One hears so much about personality, maturity, dominance. Instead, the gospel overflows with words like *little children* when Jesus addresses the Apostles.

To Jesus through Mary

Ask Jesus to help you to personalize your love for Mary—in order to love as he loves; in order to be sources of joy, as he is; in order to be closer to her, as he is; in order to share with her everything, even the cross.

Every one of us must carry his or her own cross; it is our sign of belonging to Christ. We need Mary to help us share it.

Holiness is not a luxury but a duty. Great holiness is simple if we belong completely to Mary.

We must be very grateful to God for the burdensome trips we have undertaken in the streets, by train, by plane, by bicycle, in search of souls; for the joy we have tried to spread in the world. Let us give full freedom to the Virgin for her to use us.

APPENDIX A

O Jesus, you who suffer,
grant that today and every day I may be able to see you
in the person of your sick ones and that, by offering
them my care, I may serve you.
Grant that, even if you are hidden under the unattrac-
tive disguise
of anger, of crime, or of madness,
I may recognize you and say,
"Jesus, you who suffer, how sweet it is to serve you."
Give me, Lord, this vision of faith,
and my work will never be monotonous.
I will find joy in harboring
the small whims and desires of all the poor who suffer.
Dear sick one, you are still more beloved to me
because you represent Christ.
What a privilege I am granted in being able to take care
of you!
O God, since you are Jesus who suffers,
deign to be for me also
a Jesus who is patient, indulgent with my faults,
who only looks at my intentions,
which are to love you and to serve you
in the person of each of these children of yours who
suffer.
Lord, increase my faith.
Bless my efforts and my work,
now and forever.

Some Chronological Facts of Mother Teresa's Life

August 27, 1910

Agnes Gonxha is born in Skopje, Albania (Yugoslavia). She has two sisters and one brother.

November 28, 1928

She enters the Sisters of Our Lady of Loreto, at the mother house of Rathfarnham, Ireland.

1929

She is sent to India to do her novitiate at Darjeeling. She desires to be a missionary. After taking her religious vows, she begins teaching at St. Mary's High School in Calcutta. For some years she holds the position of director of curriculum. She is also in charge of the Daughters of St. Anne, an Indian religious congregation attached to the Sisters of Our Lady of Loreto.

September 10, 1946

Mother Teresa defines this as the "Day of Inspiration": while traveling by train to a retreat, she receives the inspiration to devote herself completely to the service of the poorest poor. She asks permission from her superiors and from the archbishop of Calcutta to leave the convent and work in the poor neighborhoods of the city among the forsaken and the dying.

August 8, 1948

She receives permission from Rome to leave the Sisters of Our Lady of Loreto and to devote herself to a mission among the poor. She takes an intensive nursing course with the Missionary Physician Sisters in Patna. By Christmas she is already in Calcutta, devoted to her mission and temporarily a guest of the Sisters of the Poor.

December 21, 1948

She obtains permission to open her first school in a poor neighborhood. It is an open-air school, in a public park, for children who are in more need of learning basic hygiene than of learning the alphabet.

February 1949

A European family residing in Calcutta offers her the garret of their house.

March 19, 1949

The first vocation comes: a young woman, who was once a student of Mother Teresa, wants to lead the same life as her teacher.

October 7, 1950

The Missionaries of Charity is born in Calcutta. To the three traditional vows they add the vow to devote themselves permanently and exclusively to the poorest poor, without ever accepting any material rewards for their work. From Calcutta the congregation soon spreads to other places in India.

March 25, 1963

The congregation of the Missionary Brothers of Charity is born, inspired by the work of Mother Teresa and fostered by Brother Andrew, an Australian Jesuit missionary working in Calcutta.

February 1, 1965

Pope Paul VI grants pontifical approval to Mother Teresa's congregation. The same year sees the establishment of the first foundation outside India, in Caracas and Barquisimeto, Venezuela.

1967-1969

Houses are opened in Ceylon, Tanzania, Rome, and Australia to care for the poor people of the most destitute neighborhoods.

March 26, 1969

Pope Paul VI approves the Association of Coworkers of Mother Teresa as an affiliate to the Missionaries of Charity but with its own statutes.

1970

Mother Teresa establishes new foundations in Australia, Jordan, and London, where the novitiate of the Missionaries of Charity for American and European aspirants is constituted.

January 6, 1971

From the hands of Pope Paul VI she receives the John XXIII International Prize for Peace. She also receives the Good Samaritan Prize in Boston. During that same year she opens new foundations in New York, Belfast, and Dacca, Bangladesh.

1972

From the Indian government, which has already awarded her the highest degree of the Order of the Lotus, she receives the Pandit Nehru Prize for international understanding. That same year she opens houses in Israel and the Mauritius Islands.

May 1973

The first Spanish biographies of Mother Teresa are published, proposing the creation of a group of co-workers of Mother Teresa in Spain. The same year Mother Teresa receives from the hands of the Prince of Edinburgh the Templeton Prize, for which she has been unanimously selected from among two thousand candidates of various nationalities and religions, by a jury of representatives from ten world religious groups. The award is motivated by the quality of her religious witness.

1974

New foundations in Lima, Peru; Addis Ababa, Ethiopia; and Catherine, Australia.

1975

Mother Teresa, representing the Holy See, attends the world conference in Mexico, organized by the United Nations to mark the International Year of Women. From the United Nations Food and Agriculture Organization she receives the Albert Schweitzer Prize "as a token of gratitude for her tireless commitment to the hungry and to the poor of the whole world."

October 7, 1975

The Missionaries of Charity, which is experiencing a constant increase in vocations, celebrates its silver anniversary. All the religious groups in India are eager to join in this event.

January 8, 1976

Opening of a third foundation in Bombay, called *Asha Dan* (Gift of Hope).

February 2, 1976

A new center is opened in Sanaa, Yemen, with a school for children and adults and sewing classes for girls.

February 23, 1976

Benedictine monks of the Camaldolese Order give to the Missionaries of Charity the monastery of St. Gregory in Mount Celio, Rome. The sisters destined it to be a house for the dying (with fifty beds) and for abandoned people who have been picked up during the night in the surroundings of the Termini station.

March 25, May 31, July 15, 1976

Openings of new assistance centers and foundations of the Missionaries of Charity in the following Indian localities: Jaipalguri, Chandigarh, and Baruipur.

April 8, 1976

Two centers are opened in Mexico City: one for the abandoned dying, the other for abandoned orphans.

April 26, 1976

A center is opened to offer aid to those left homeless after the earthquake that shook Guatemala on February 4 of the same year.

June 3, 1976

Mother Teresa visits Spain for the first time, after receiving an invitation to establish an assistance center there. In a stay of twenty-four hours during a trip from New York to Calcutta, she finds time to answer questions in a press conference, to be interviewed on radio and television, to lay the groundwork and confirm the members of the association of Co-workers of Mother Teresa in Spain, to attend two religious activities, and to visit the slums of Madrid. Asked about her decision to open one or several assistance centers of the Missionaries of Charity in Spain, Mother Teresa answered, "Yes, I have seen that there are urgent needs. But do not wait till we come before you start working. Right now we have eighty-four requests like the one you have made us, to establish foundations."

June 13, 1976

On the feast of the Sacred Heart of Jesus, and with the participation of the Cardinal Archbishop of New York, the establishment of a new, more expressly contemplative branch of the Sisters of Mother Teresa takes place. These are the Sisters of the Word, whose mission is to "live the

Word of God through eucharistic adoration, contemplation, and the proclamation of the Word to the people of God, in order to carry, with Mary, Mother of the Church, the Word made flesh, in order for that Word to remain in the hearts of men."

August 1-8, 1976

Mother Teresa is invited by the organizers of the Forty-first International Eucharistic Congress, held in Philadelphia, to participate in a symposium on hunger, together with Dom Helder Camara and Fathers Pedro Arrupe and Bernhard Haring. (Mother Teresa's address there is the first chapter of this book.) Also on this occasion, she takes part in a series of lectures on the topic "Women and the Eucharist," together with Dorothy Day, Rosemary Goldie, and Eileen Eagan. (Her address is the second chapter of this book.)

August 17, 1976

Meeting in Taize, France, with fifteen thousand young people from various Christian confessions.

December 31, 1976

Detailed statistical data concerning the Missionaries of Charity: Houses in India: 66. Houses in other countries: 34. Number of religious sisters (including professed sisters, novices, postulants, and aspirants): 1,343. Total number of schools, shelters, leper houses, clinics, houses for the dying, and assistance centers, in India and elsewhere: 729. Number of pupils, sheltered orphans, lepers, dying people, and patients in general: 6,544,864.

June 10, 1977

From the hands of Prince Philip of Edinburgh, Chancellor of the University, she receives the *honoris causa* doctorate in Theology of Cambridge University.

August 5, 1977

A new center is opened in Haiti.

August 15, 1977

Mother Teresa opens a center for assistance and service to the poorest poor in Rotterdam, the most industrialized city of Holland.

November 1, 1977

Twenty-fifth anniversary of the founding of the first *Nirmal Hriday* (House of the Abandoned Dying) of Calcutta.

January 1978

The Missionaries of Charity open assistance centers for the poorest poor in Argentina, Lebanon, and Panama.

May 15, 1979

In the Rome novitiate, the first Spanish Missionary of Charity makes her religious profession. Her first destination is Panama.

October 17, 1979

Nobel Prize for Peace.

June 21, 1980

Opening of the first center of the Missionaries of Charity in Spain, in Madrid.

June 27, 1980

Opening of a center in Skopje, Yugoslavia, native town of Mother Teresa.

Other Books of Interest from Servant Publications

Jesus, the Word to Be Spoken
Mother Teresa

Let the words and example of Mother Teresa of Calcutta lead you each day into a closer relationship with God. This pocket guide to daily prayer and meditation is rich spiritual fare for all who are serious about following Jesus Christ. *$4.95*

One Heart Full of Love
Mother Teresa

One Heart Full of Love gathers together stirring addresses and interviews given by Mother Teresa to her Missionaries of Charity and other groups world-wide on such topics as self-giving, the call to love our neighbor, spiritual poverty in the West, and a life of joy-filled sacrifice. Here is spiritual food that will nourish your heart and soul. *$4.95*

Servant Publications • Dept. 209 • P.O. Box 7455
Ann Arbor, Michigan 48107
Please include payment plus $1.25 per book
for postage and handling.
*Send for our FREE catalog of Christian
books, music, and cassettes.*